Cobourg Ontario Book 4 in Colour Photos, Saving Our History One Photo at a Time

Photography
by Barbara Raué
©2019

Series Name: Cruising Ontario

Book 228: Cobourg Book 4

Cover photo: 178 Perry Street, Page 8

Series Name: Cruising Ontario
Saving Our History One Photo at a Time
in colour photos

Books Available in Alphabetical Order:
Aberfoyle, Acton, Ajax, Alton, Amherstburg, Ancaster, Arthur, Auburn, Aylmer, Ayr, Beaver Valley, Belgrave, Belleville, Bloomingdale, Blyth, Brantford, Brockville, Burford, Burlington, Caledon, Caledonia, Cambridge, Carlow, Chatsworth, Clifford, Collingwood, Conestogo, Delhi, Dorchester to Aylmer, Drayton, Drumbo, Dundas, Dunlop, Eden Mills, Elmira, Elora, Erin, Essex, Fergus, Goderich, Grimsby, Guelph, Hagersville, Hamilton, Hanover, Harriston, Hespeler, Jarvis, Kingston, Kingsville, Kitchener, Lake Superior, Lincoln, Linwood, Listowel, London, Lucknow, Merrickville, Mono, Mount Forest, Mount Pleasant, Neustadt, New Hamburg, Newboro, Newport, Niagara-on-the-Lake, Niagara Falls, North Bay, Oakville, Onondaga, Orangeville, Orillia, Oshawa, Owen Sound, Palmerston, Paris, Pelham, Perth, Peterborough, Petrolia, Pickering, Port Colborne, Port Elgin, Portland, Preston, Rockwood, Sarnia, Sault Ste. Marie, Seaforth, Sheffield, Shelburne, Simcoe, Smiths Falls, Smithville, Southampton, St. Catharines, St. George, St. Jacobs, St. Marys, St. Thomas, Stoney Creek, Stratford, Thamesford, Thunder Bay, Tillsonburg, Toronto, Waterdown, Waterford, Waterloo, Welland, Wellesley, West Flamborough, Westport, Whitby, Windsor, Wingham, Woodstock

Book 212-215 Haldimand County
Book 216: Sudbury
Book 217: Parry Sound
Book 218-219: Uxbridge
Book 220: Port Perry

Book 221-222: Stouffville
Book 223: Colborne
Book 224: Grafton, Bolton
Book 225-230: Cobourg

Table of Contents

Cobourg is a town in Southern Ontario ninety-five kilometers (59 miles) east of Toronto and 62 kilometers (39 miles) east of Oshawa. It is located along Highway 401. To the south, Cobourg borders Lake Ontario.

The settlements that make up today's Cobourg were founded by United Empire Loyalists in 1798. The Town was originally a group of smaller villages such as Amherst and Hardscrabble, which were later named Hamilton. In 1808 it became the district town for the Newcastle District. It was renamed Cobourg in 1818, in recognition of the marriage of Princess Charlotte Augusta of Wales to Prince Leopold of Saxe-Coburg-Saalfeld (who later become King of Belgium).

By the 1830s Cobourg had become a regional center, much due to its fine harbor on Lake Ontario.

Cobourg retains its small-town atmosphere, in part due to the downtown and surrounding residential area's status as a Heritage Conservation District.

The downtown is a well-preserved example of a traditional small-town main street. Victoria Hall, the town hall completed in 1860, is a National Historic Site of Canada. The oldest building in the town is now open as the Sifton-Cook Heritage Centre and operated by the Cobourg Museum Foundation.

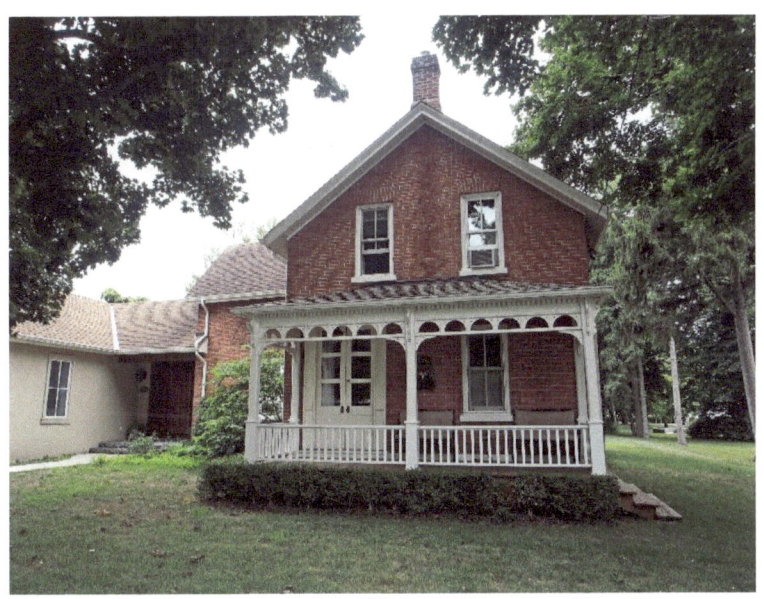

125 Perry Street – 1880s – Rooney Family

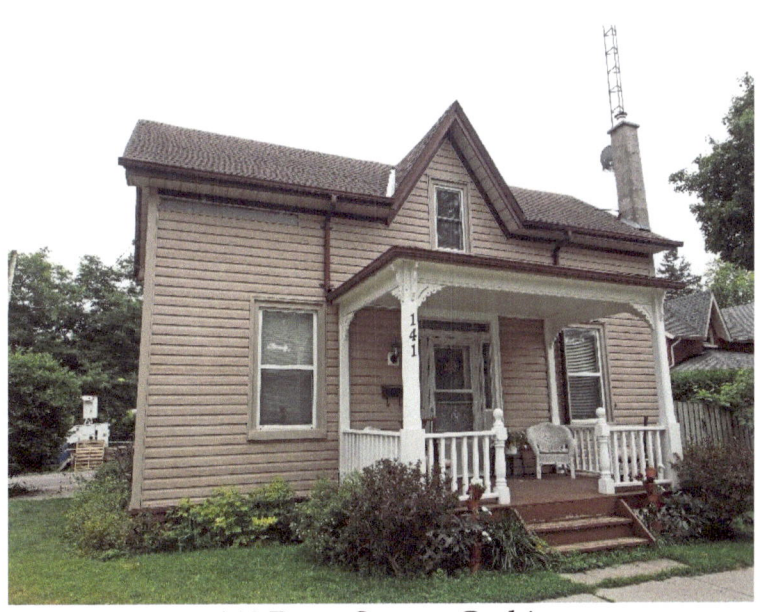

141 Perry Street - Gothic

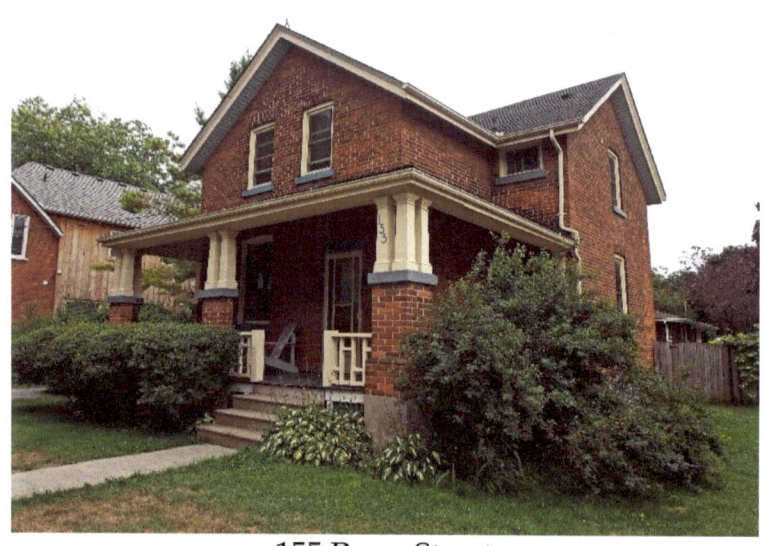

155 Perry Street

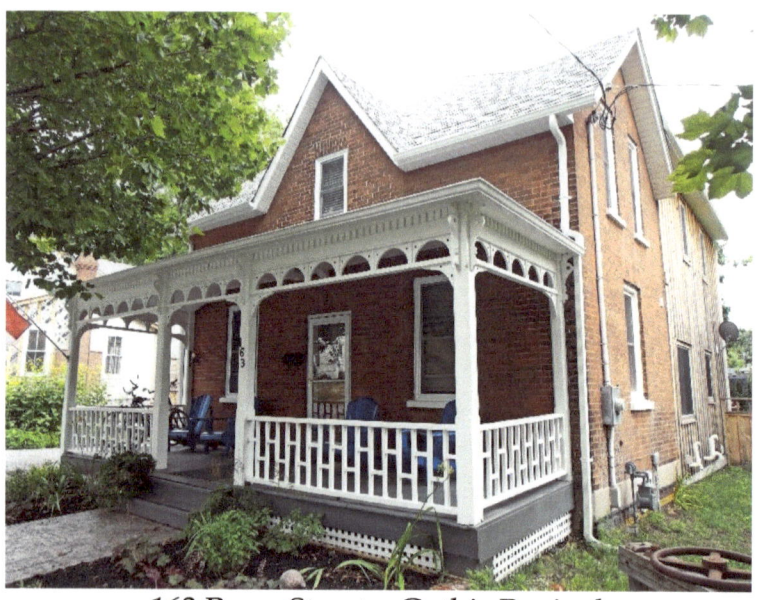

163 Perry Street – Gothic Revival

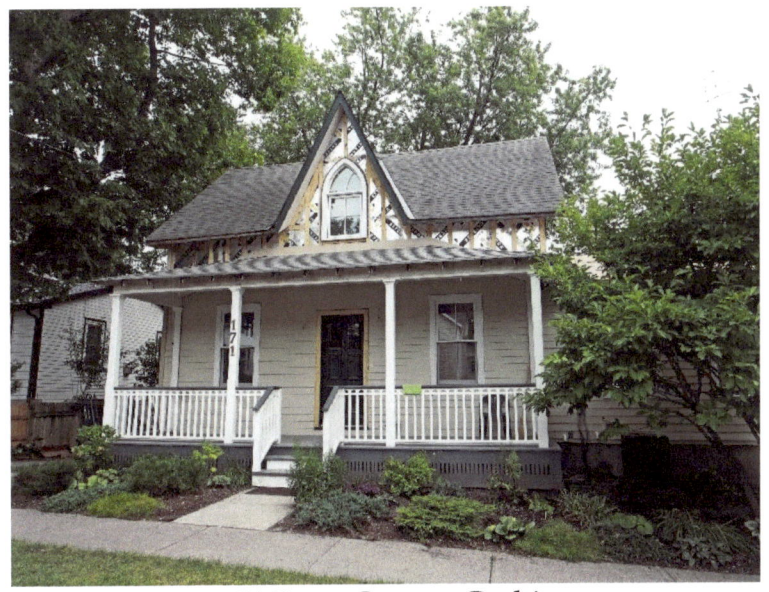

171 Perry Street - Gothic

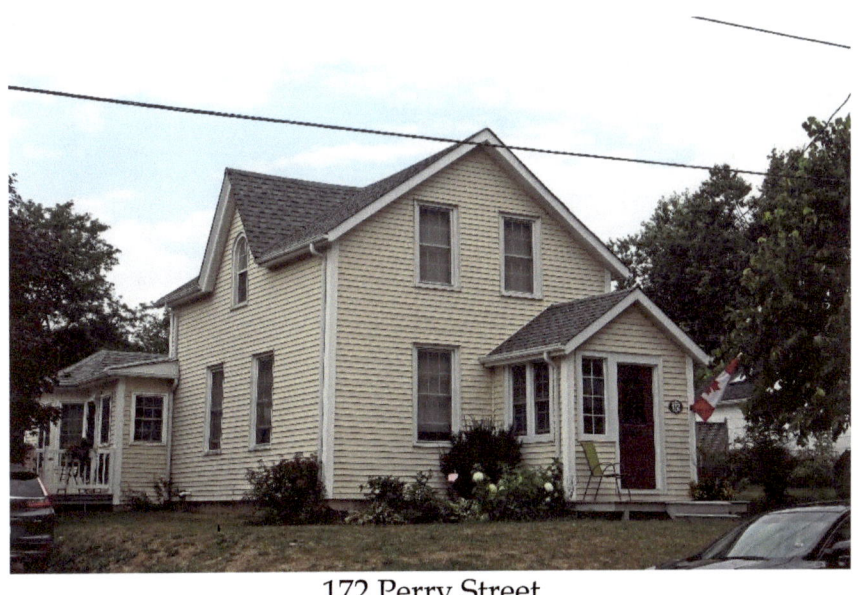

172 Perry Street

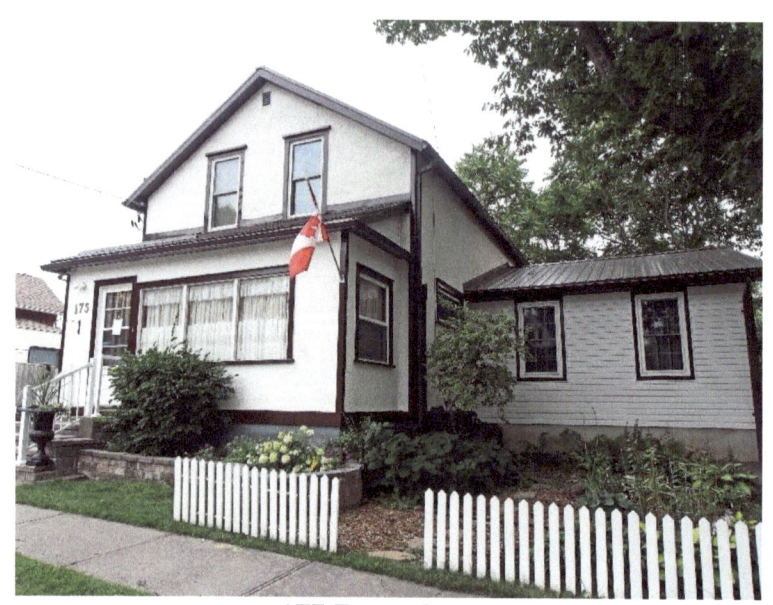

175 Perry Street

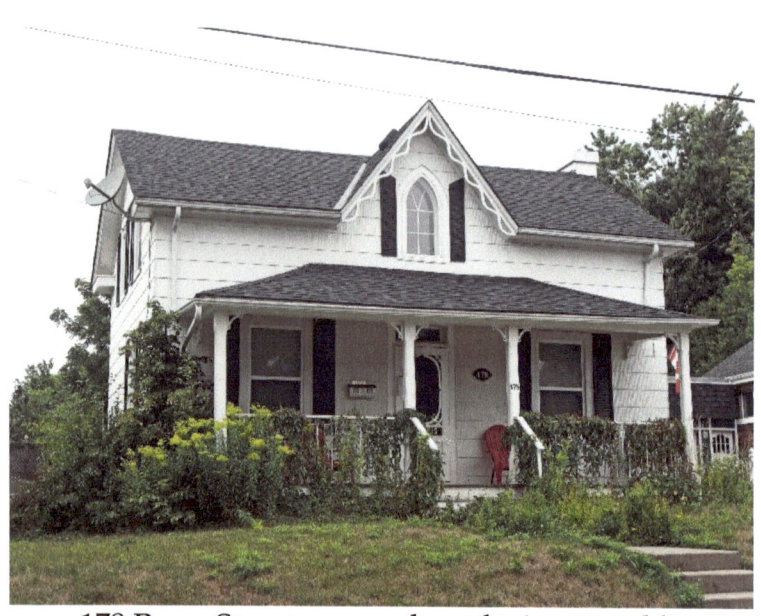

178 Perry Street – verge board trim on gable

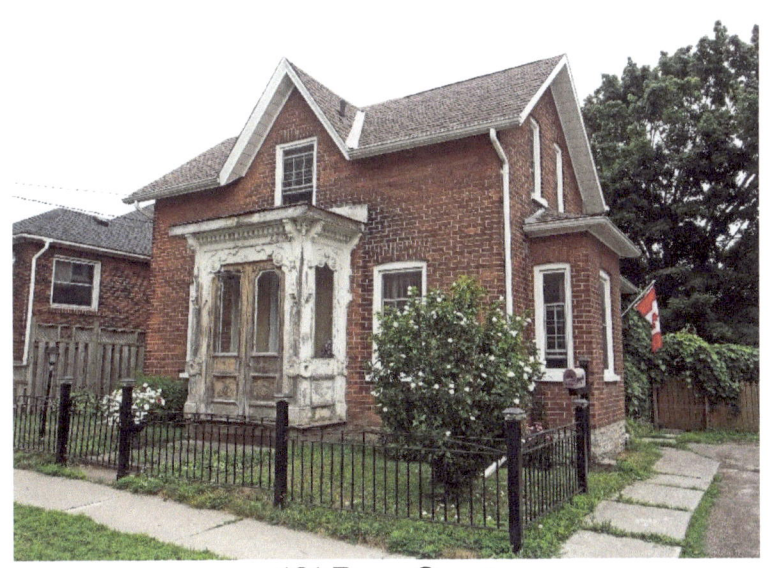

181 Perry Street

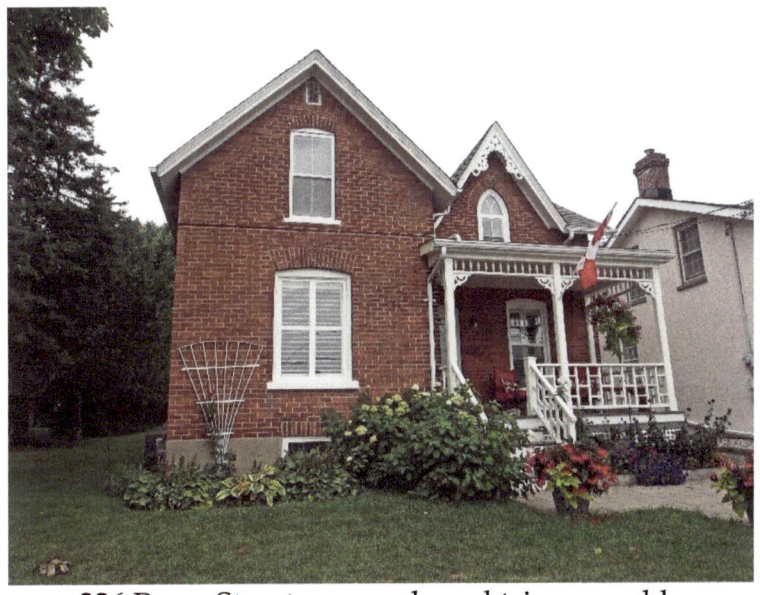

226 Perry Street – verge board trim on gable

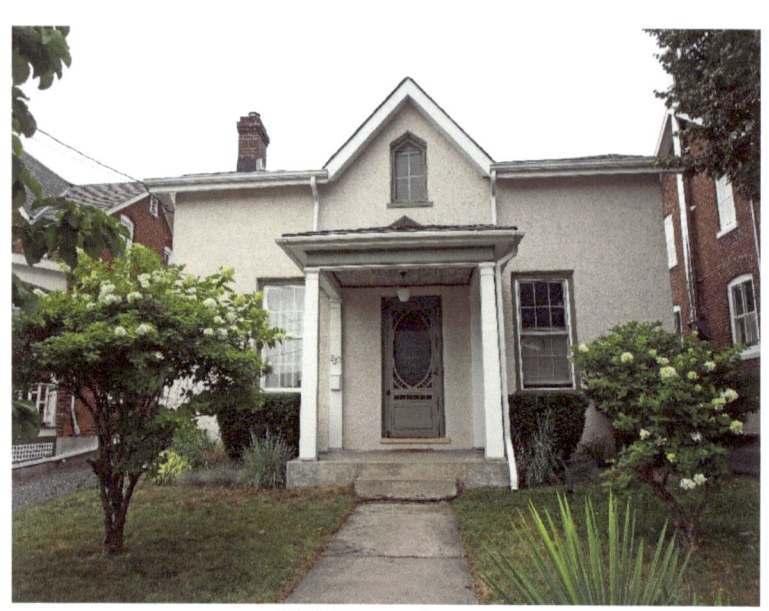

230 Perry Street

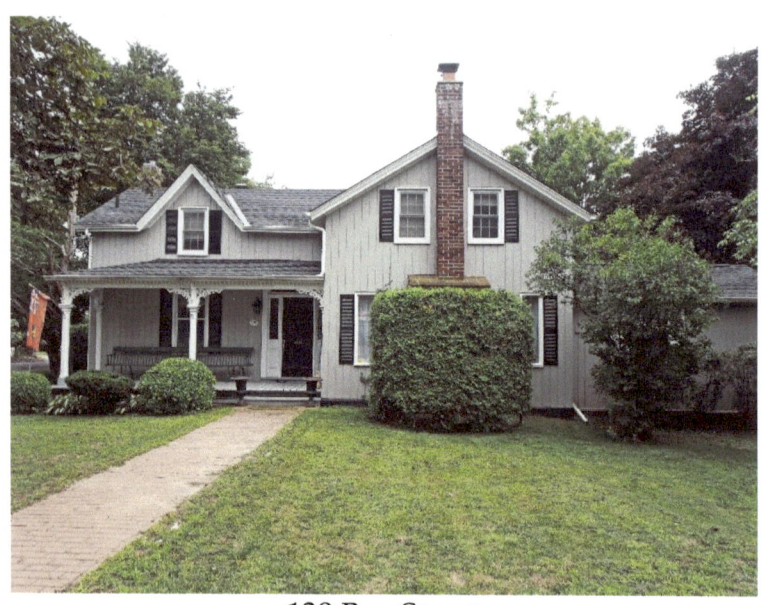

139 Bay Street

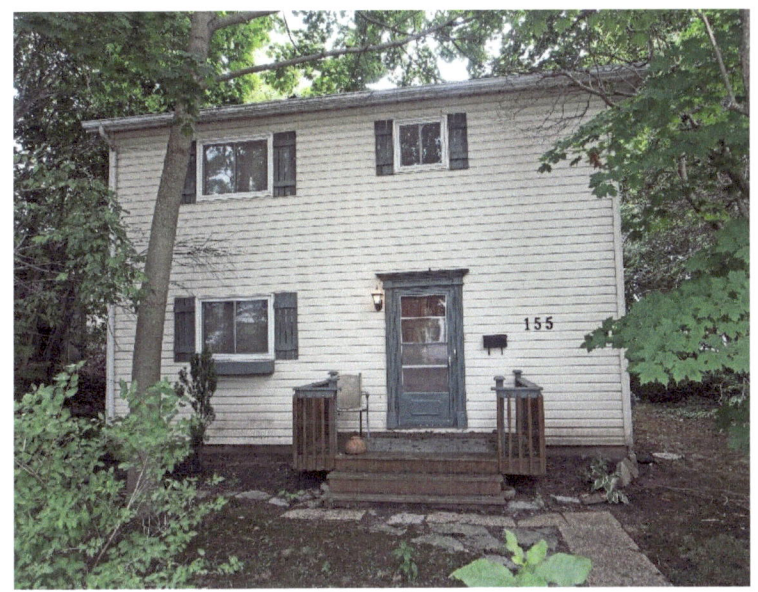

155 Bay Street

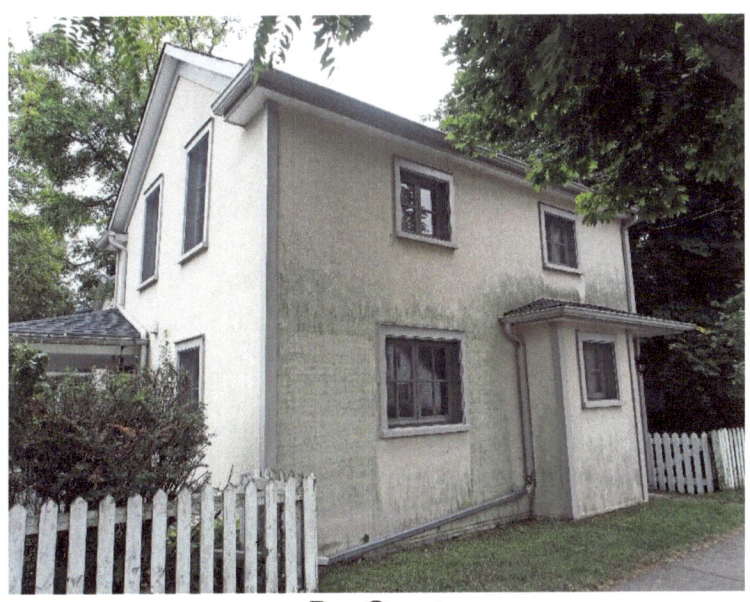

Bay Street

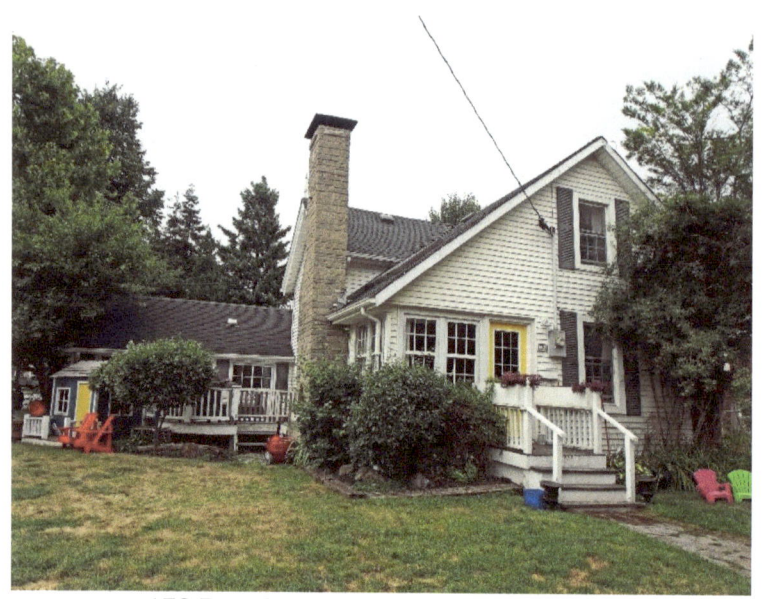

158 Bay Street – 1878 – "L" shaped

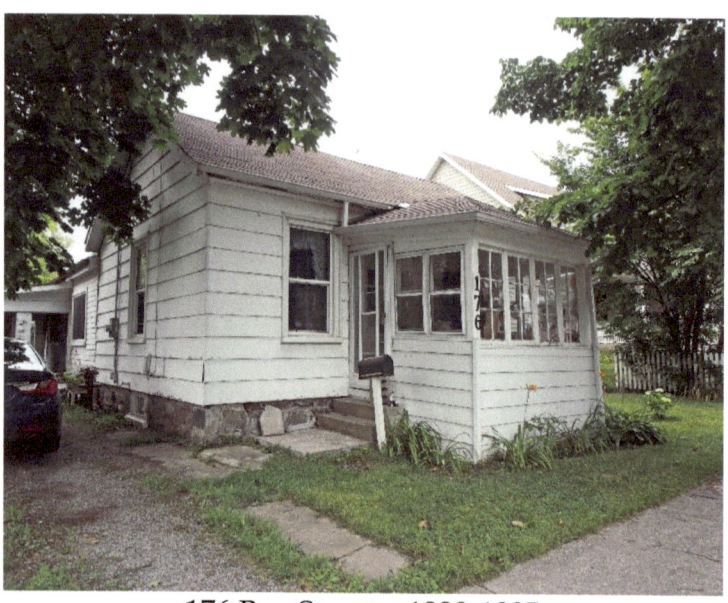

176 Bay Street – 1880-1885

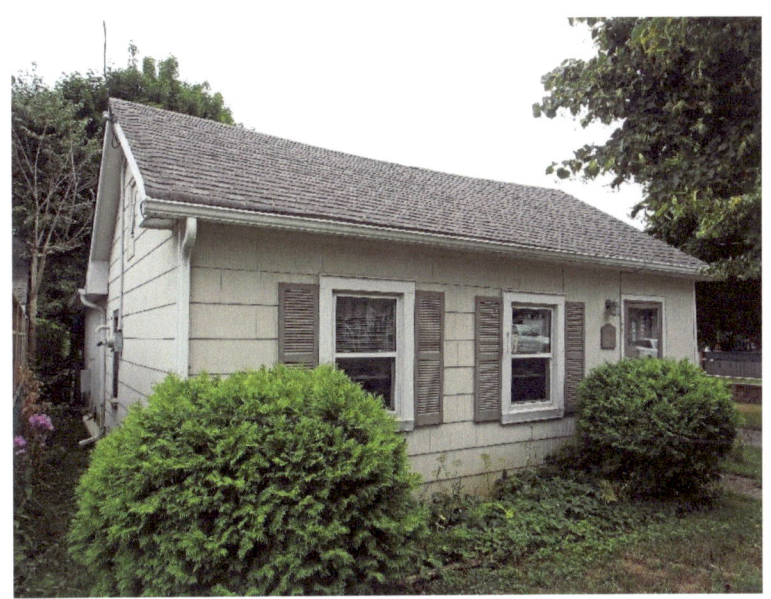

195 Bay Street - 1858

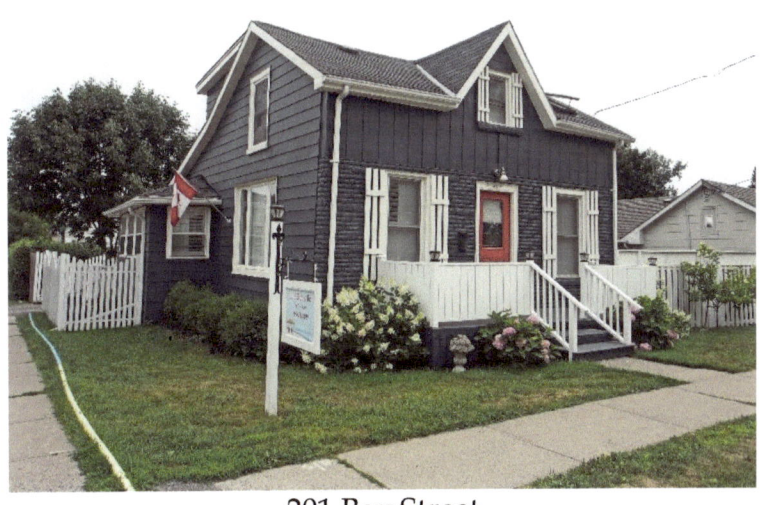

201 Bay Street

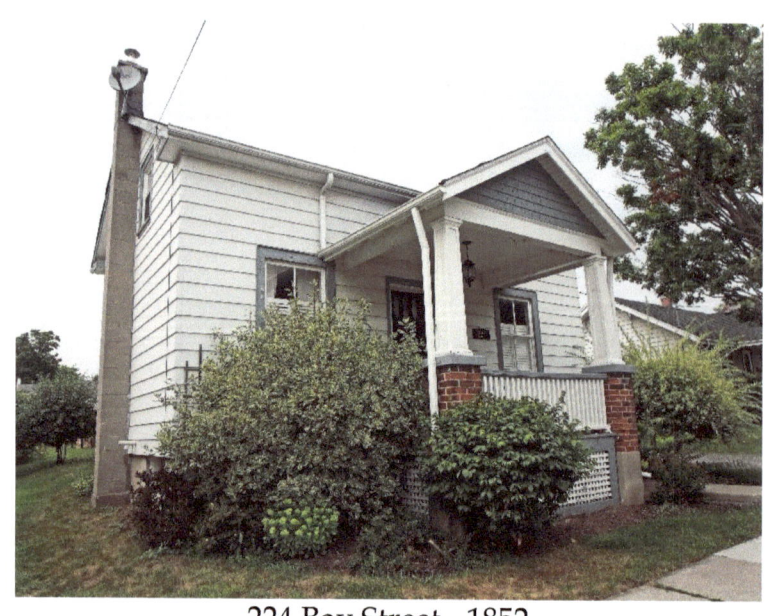

224 Bay Street - 1852

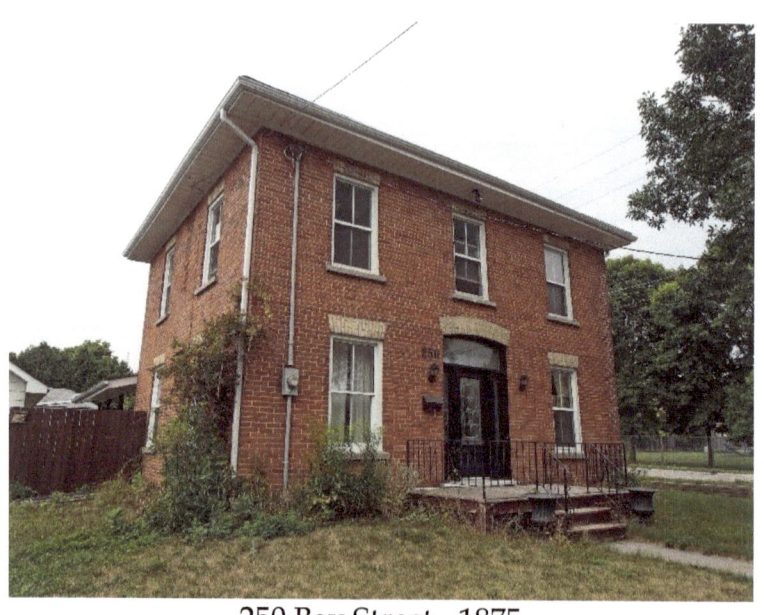

250 Bay Street - 1875

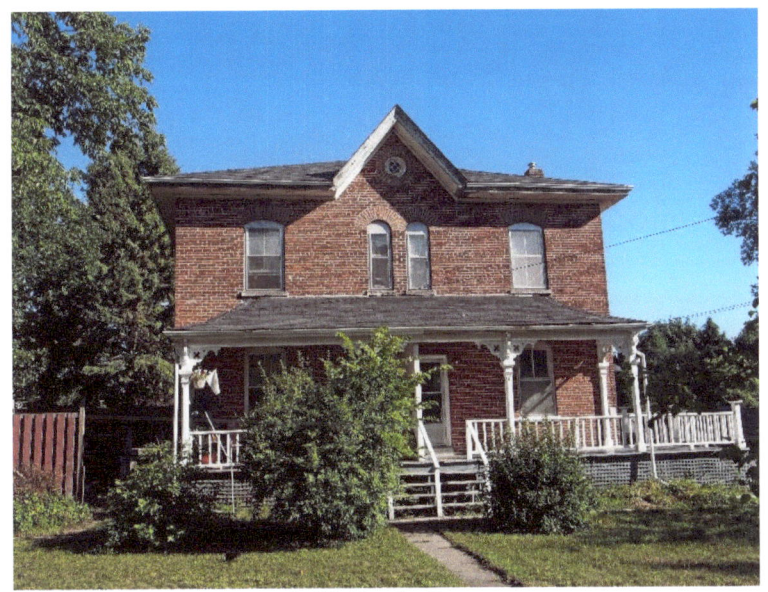

48-50 Park Street

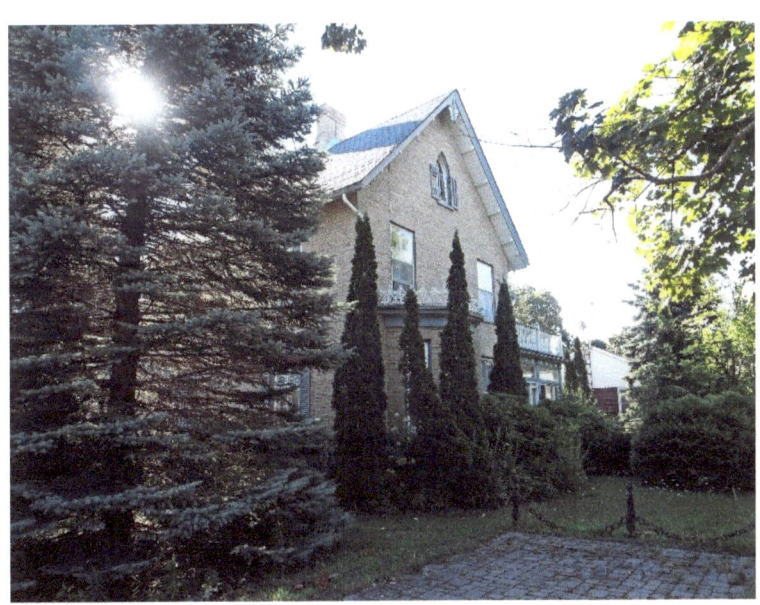

Park Street

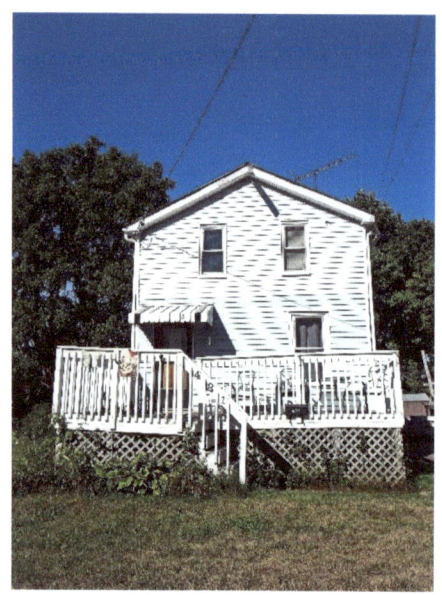

421 Roe Street

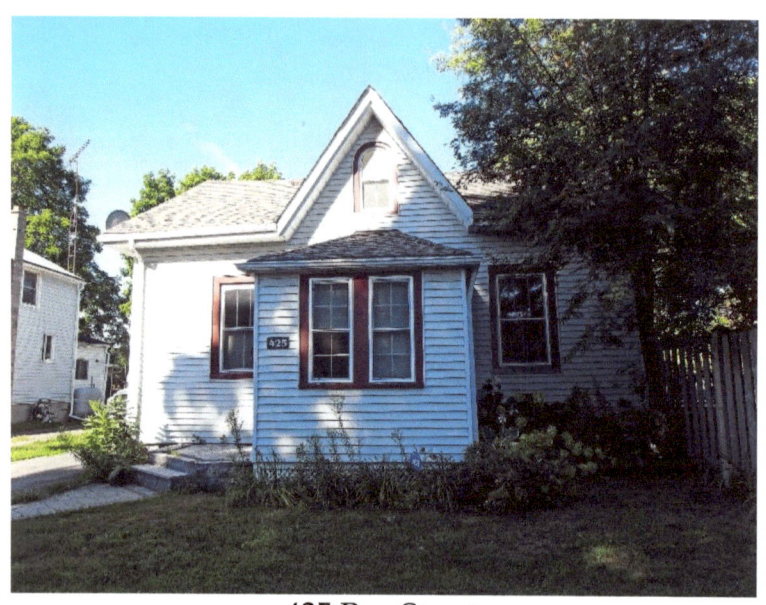

425 Roe Street

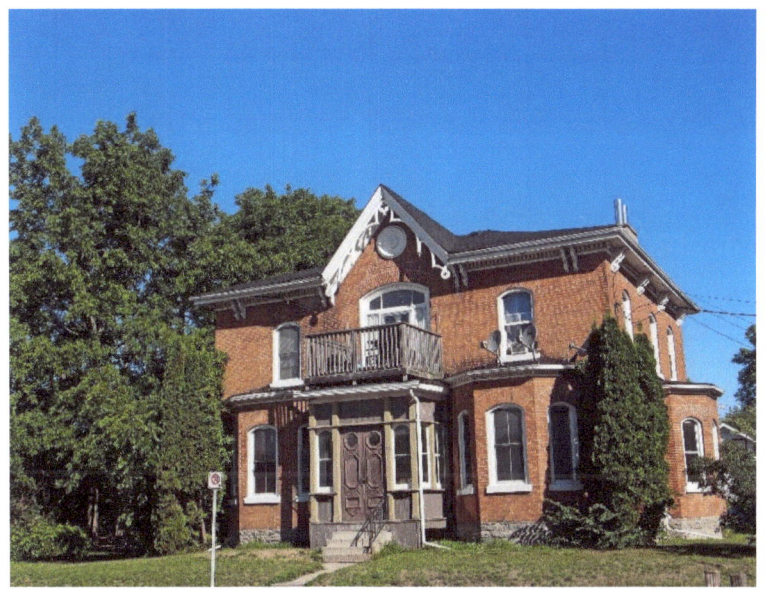

80 University Avenue West – Ontario Vernacular house – The gable apex is ornately decorated by gingerbread, under the eaves are paired brackets and a decorated frieze. There is a large wooden medallion in the center gable.

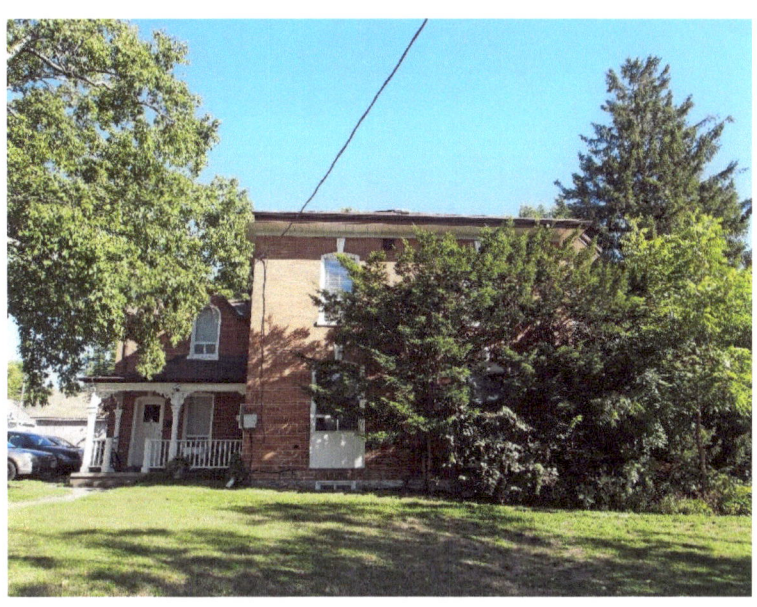

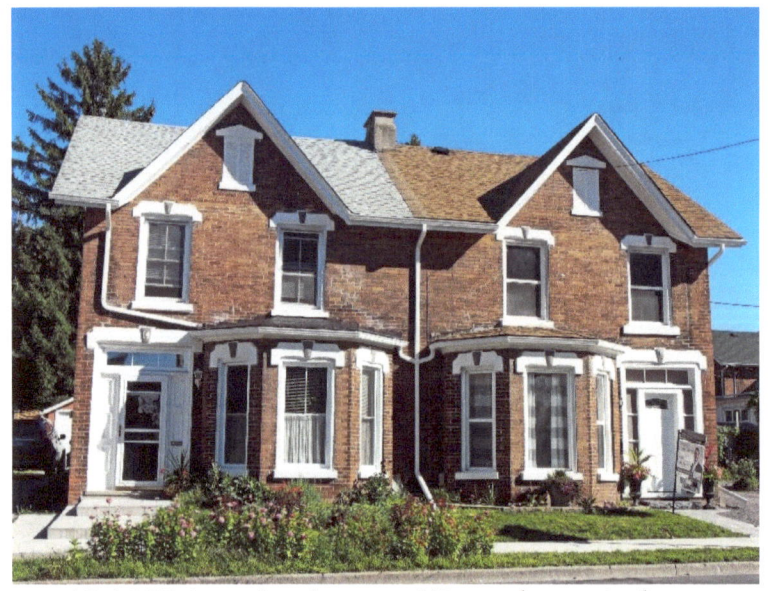

12-14 University Avenue West – bay windows

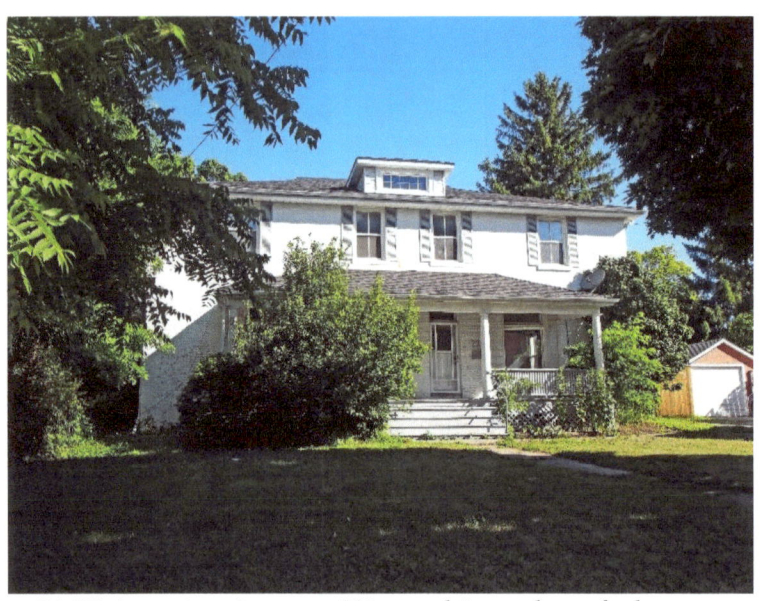

21 University Avenue West – hipped roof, dormer

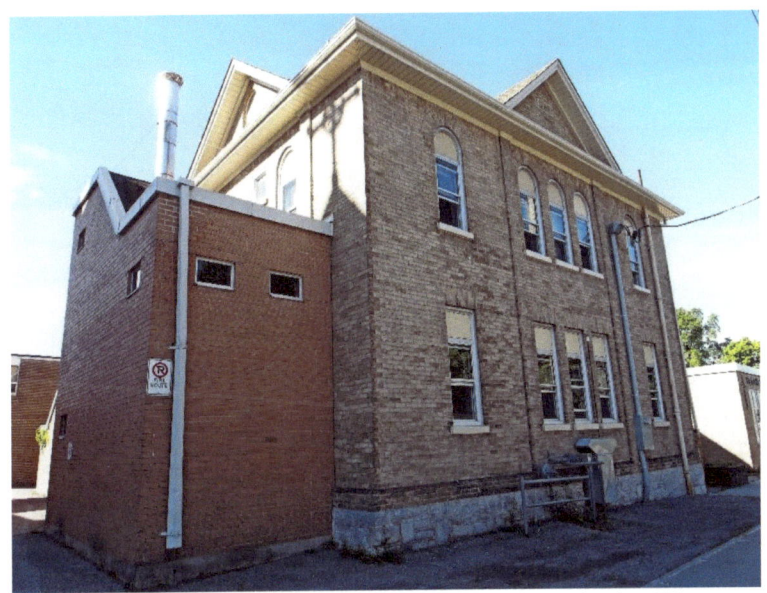

23 University Avenue West – St. Michael Catholic Elementary School

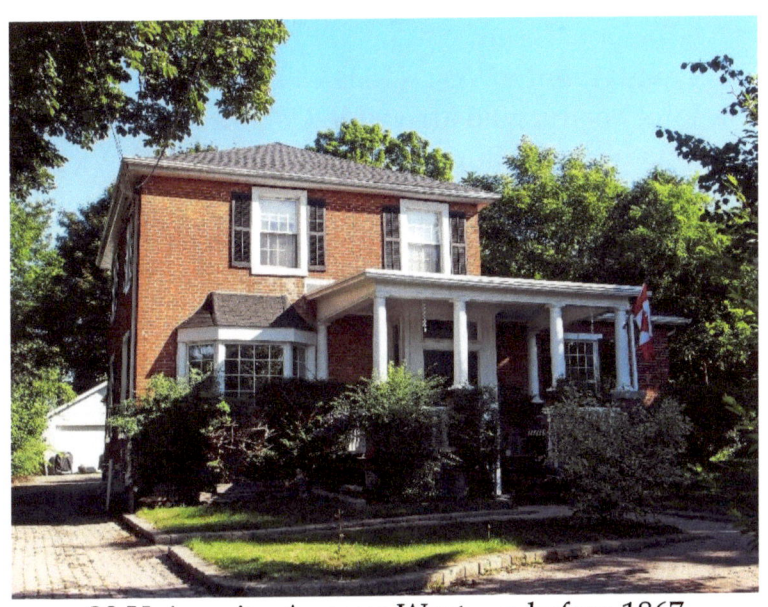

28 University Avenue West – c. before 1867

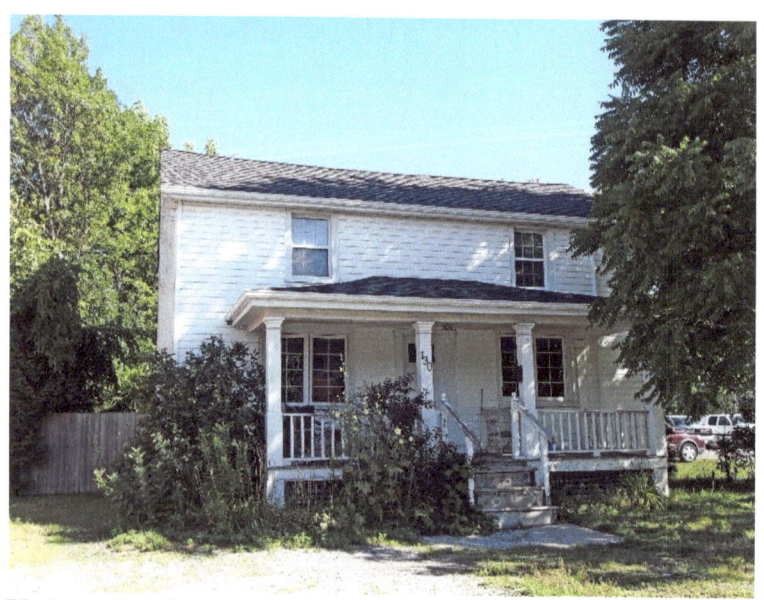

130 University Avenue West – 1834 - This house was built by the Rev. John Beatty, who arrived in Cobourg in 1833, with his son, John. Both played important roles in founding Victoria College, and John, the son, was Mayor of Cobourg five times between 1858 and 1867. The Ryerson and Beatty families were connected by marriage, as well as by the church and the college. Dr. Beatty's daughter, Emily, married her first cousin, Charles Ryerson, son of Egerton.

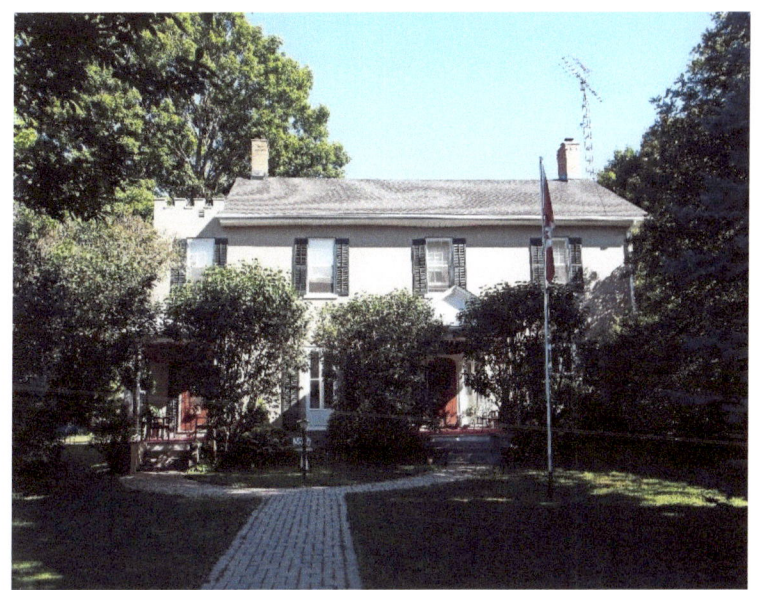

34-36 University Avenue West

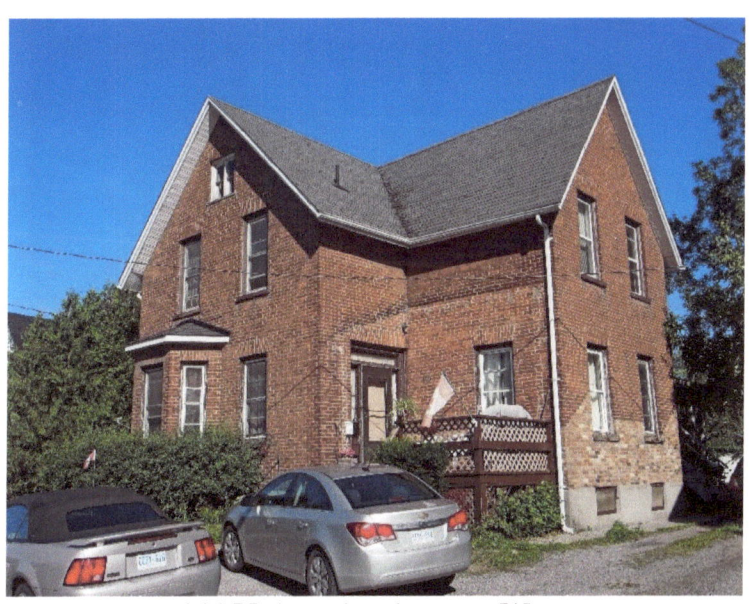

144 University Avenue West

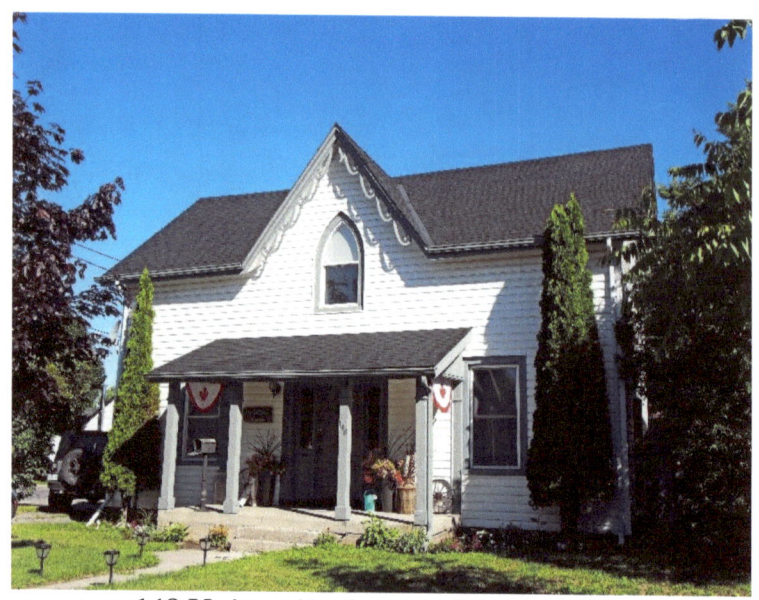

148 University Avenue West – 1850s

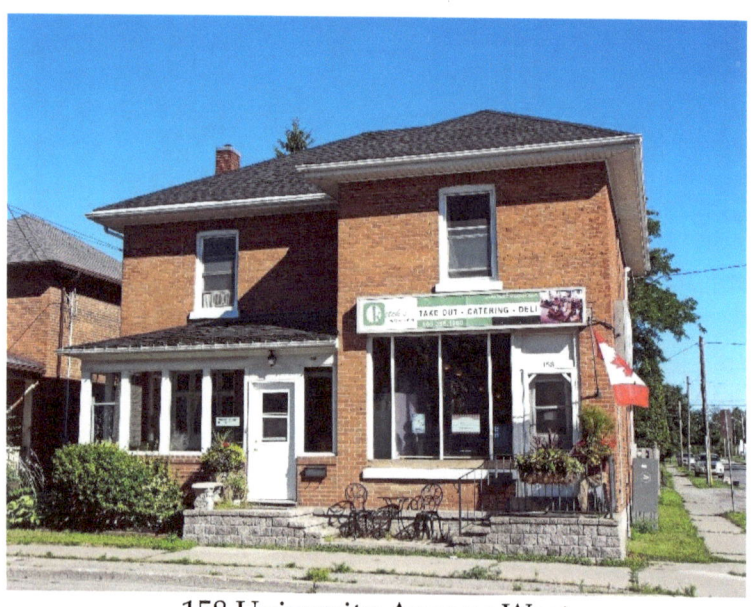

158 University Avenue West

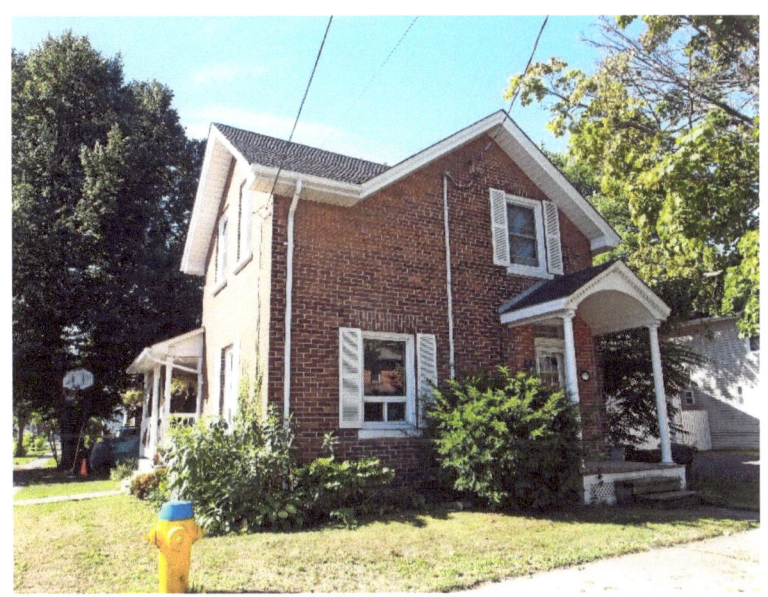

159 University Avenue West

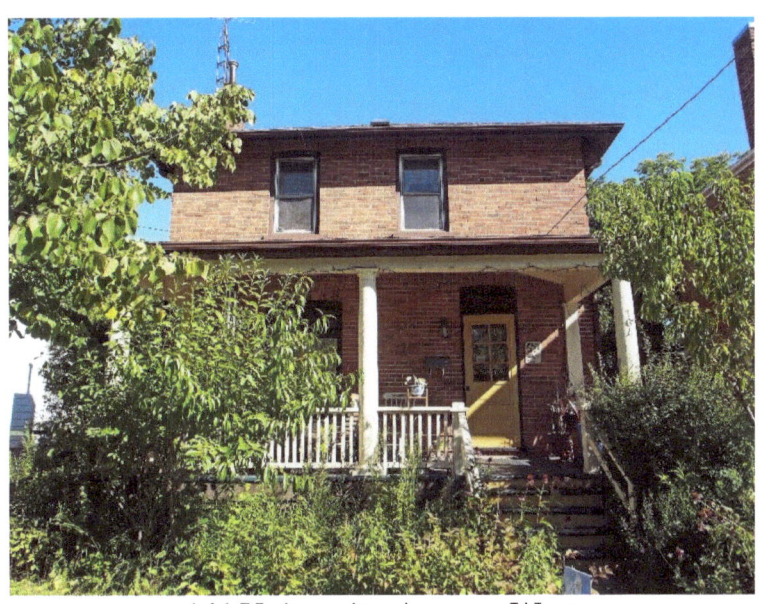

164 University Avenue West

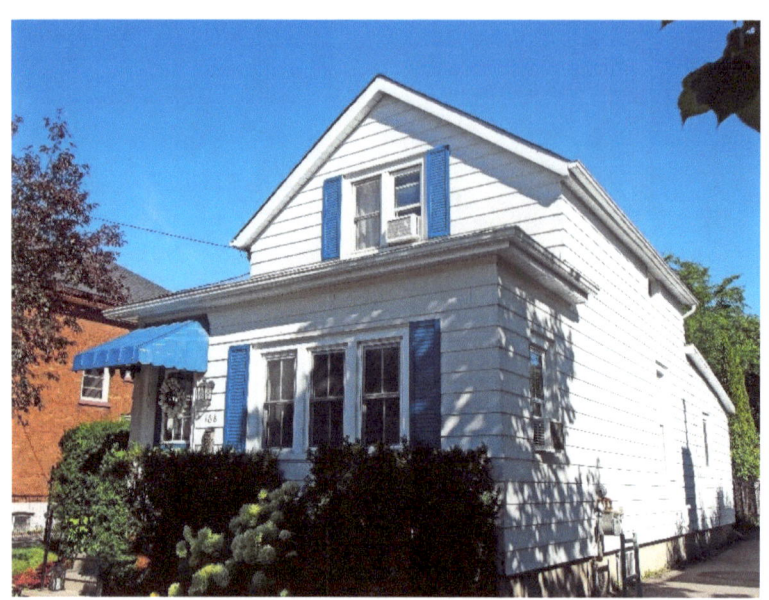

168 University Avenue West

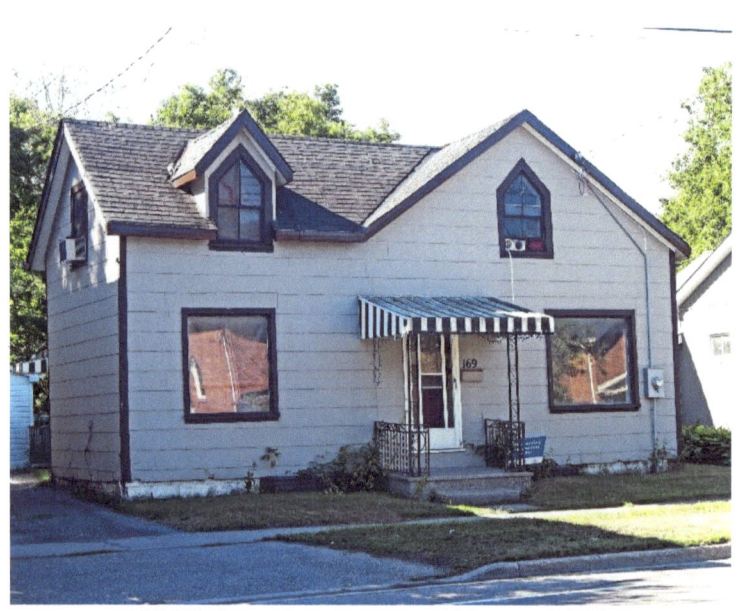

169 University Avenue West – 1860s

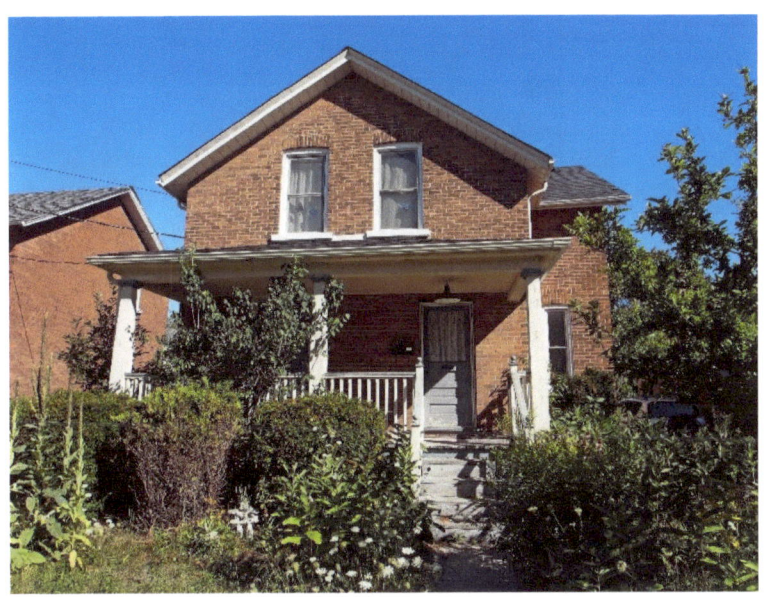

178 University Avenue West

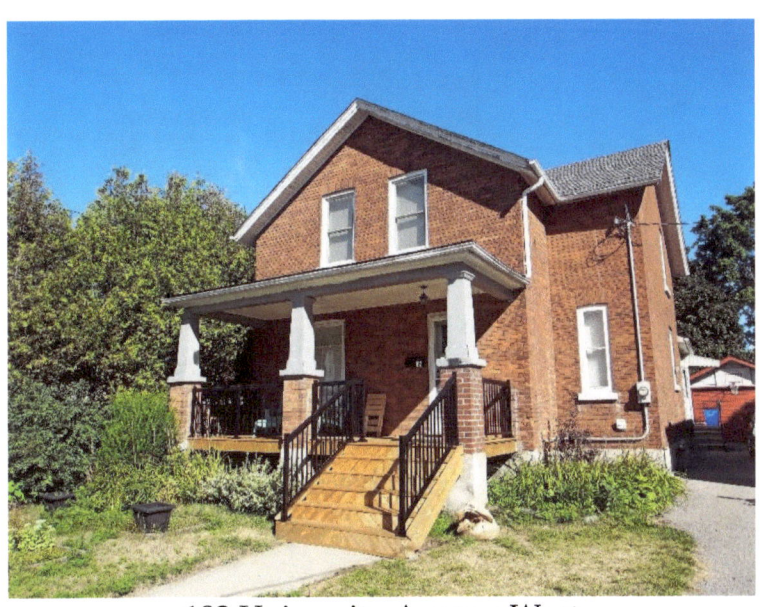

182 University Avenue West

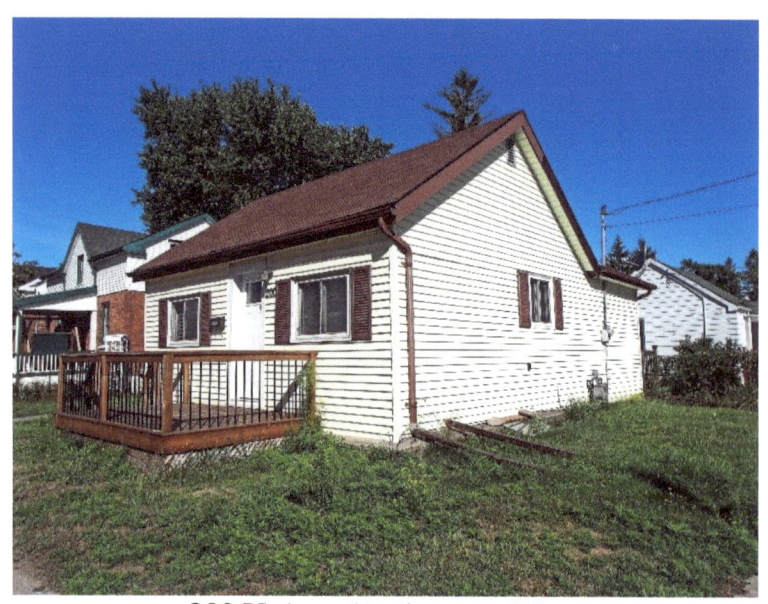

200 University Avenue West

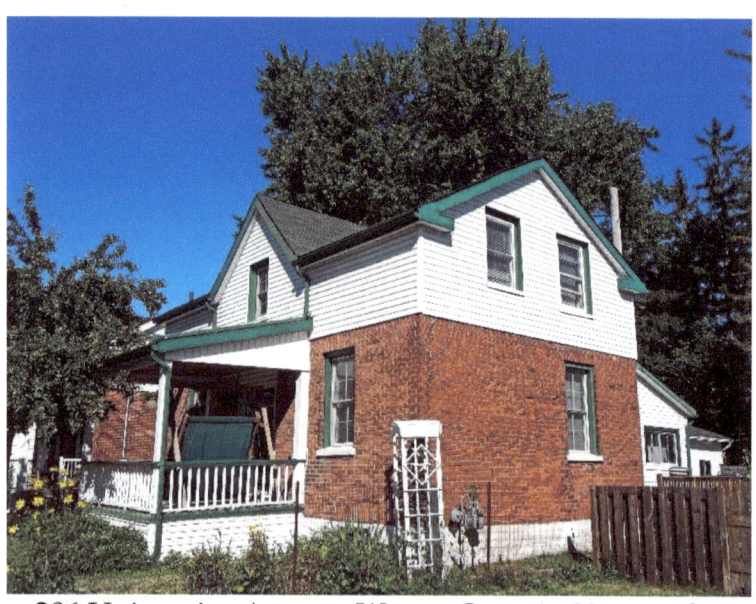

206 University Avenue West – Ontario Vernacular

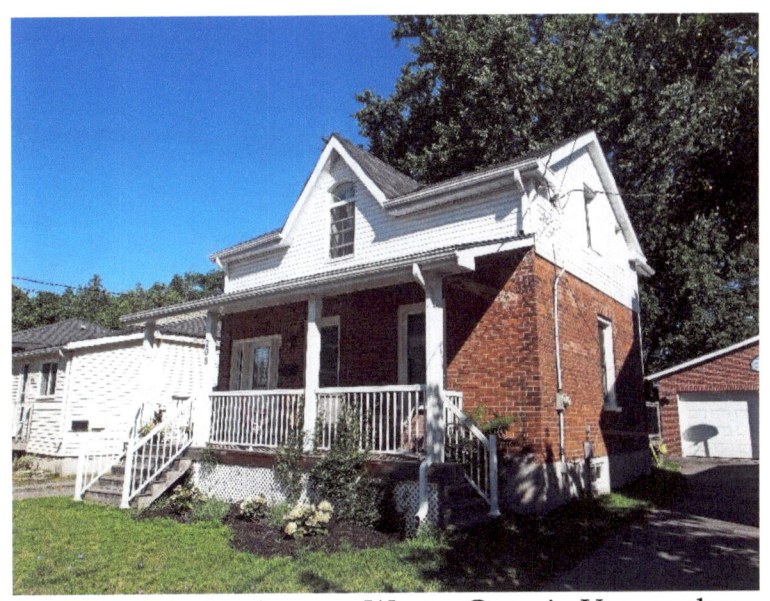

208 University Avenue West – Ontario Vernacular

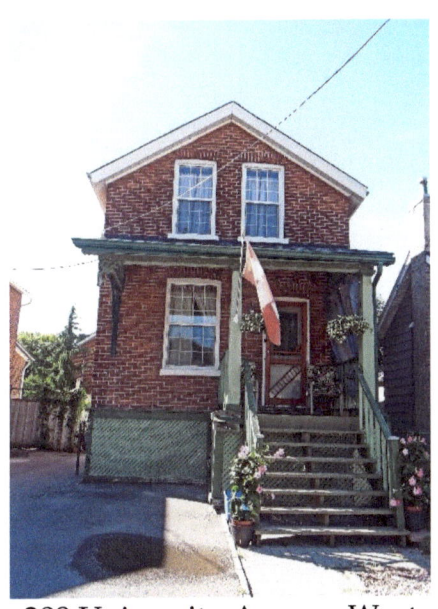

209 University Avenue West

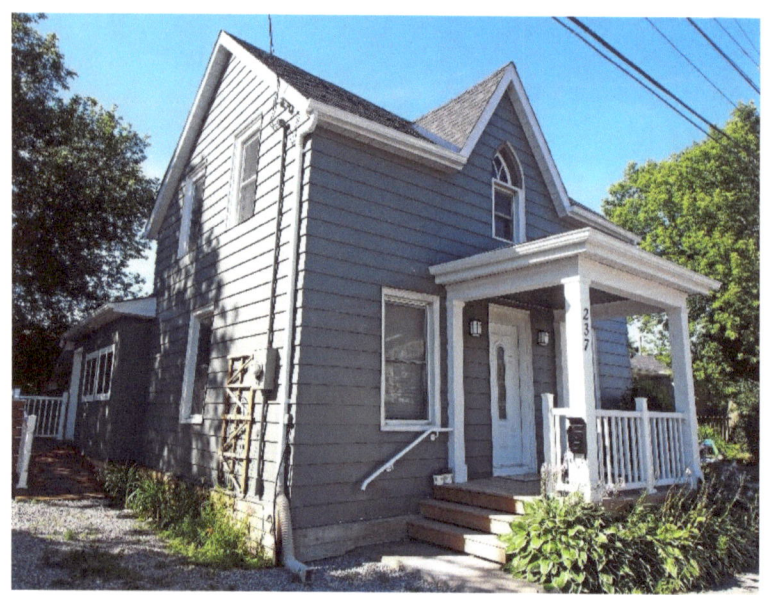

237 University Avenue West – Ontario Vernacular

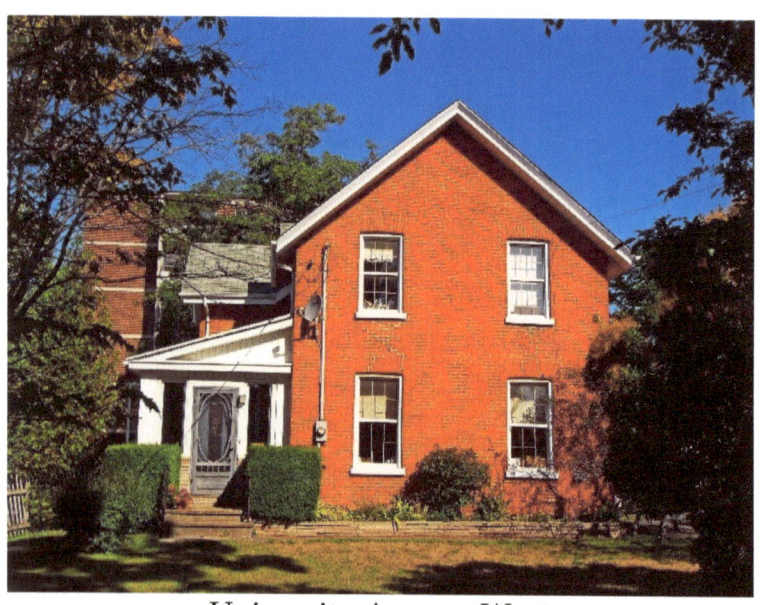

University Avenue West

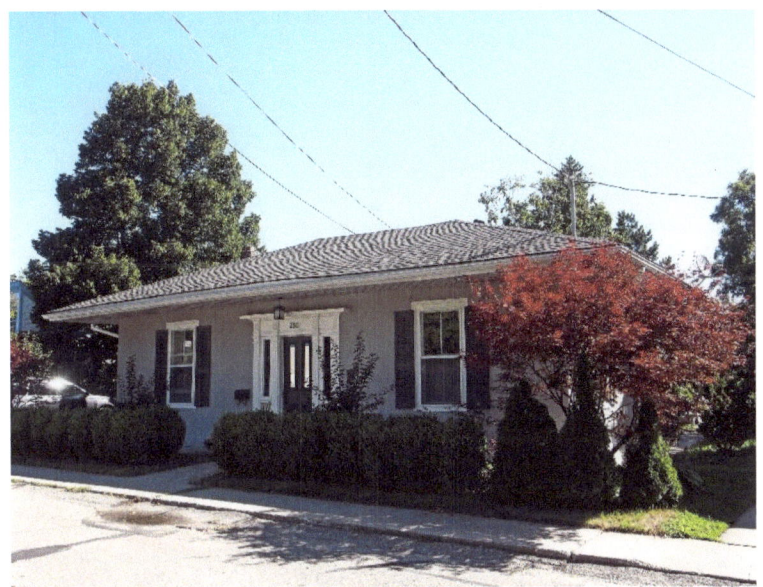

250 Mathew Street - c. 1850 - This Ontario Cottage was built by Mathew Williams. Substantial over-hanging eaves of the hipped roof give it a hat-like quality. This form of roof was unique to the Cobourg area. It has a lovely doorway.

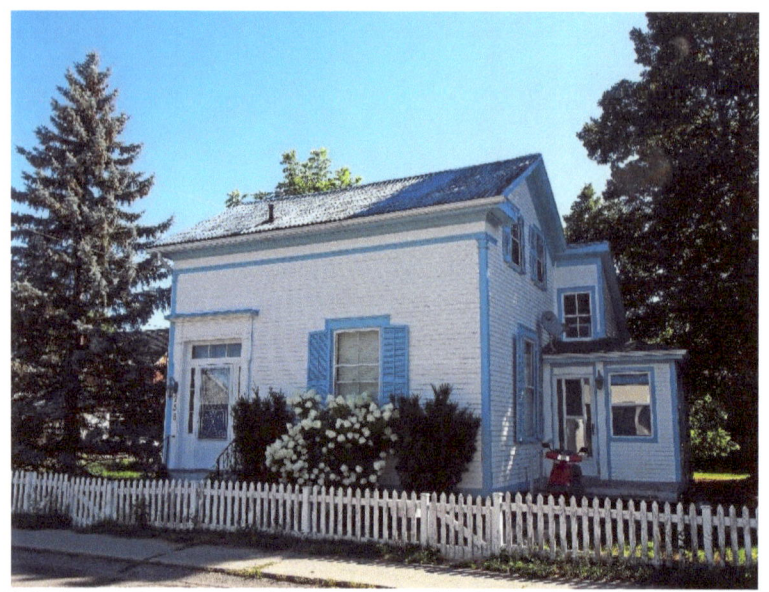

258 Mathew Street - c. 1840. -This clapboard saltbox house is stylishly finished with returning eaves and elaborate end boards. It has a splendid doorway.

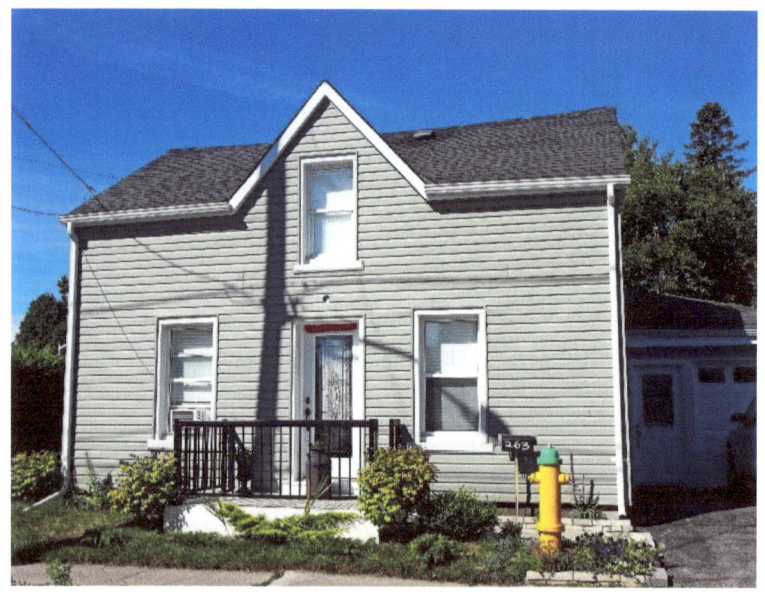

263 Mathew Street

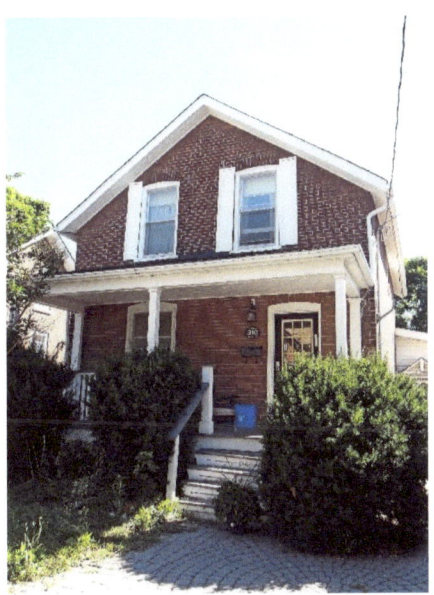

310 Mathew Street

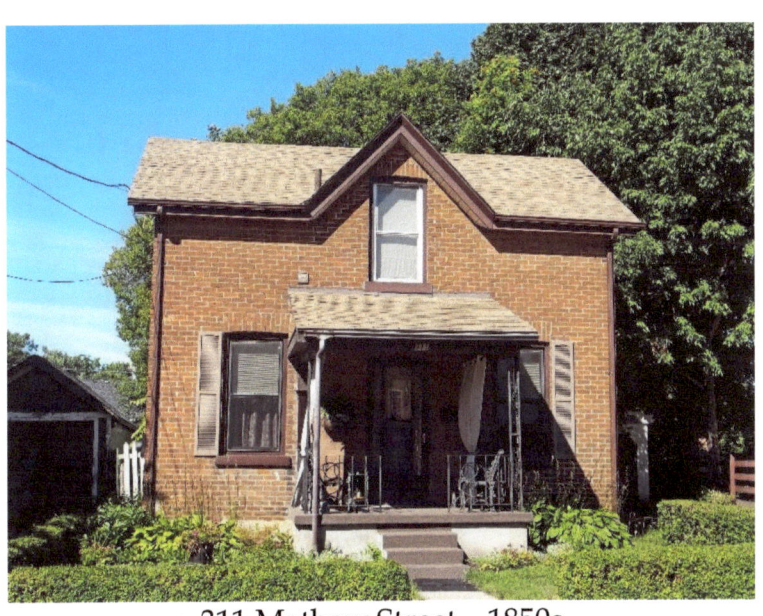

311 Mathew Street – 1850s

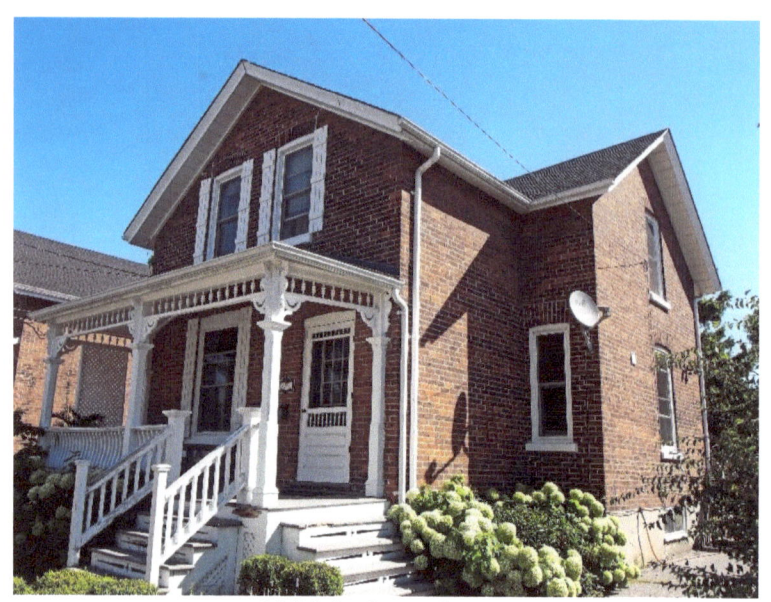

328 Mathew Street

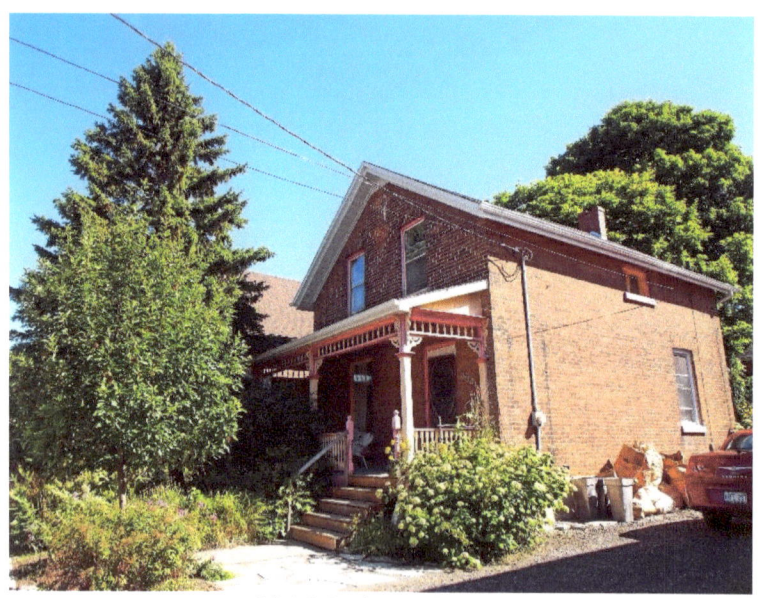

334 Mathew Street

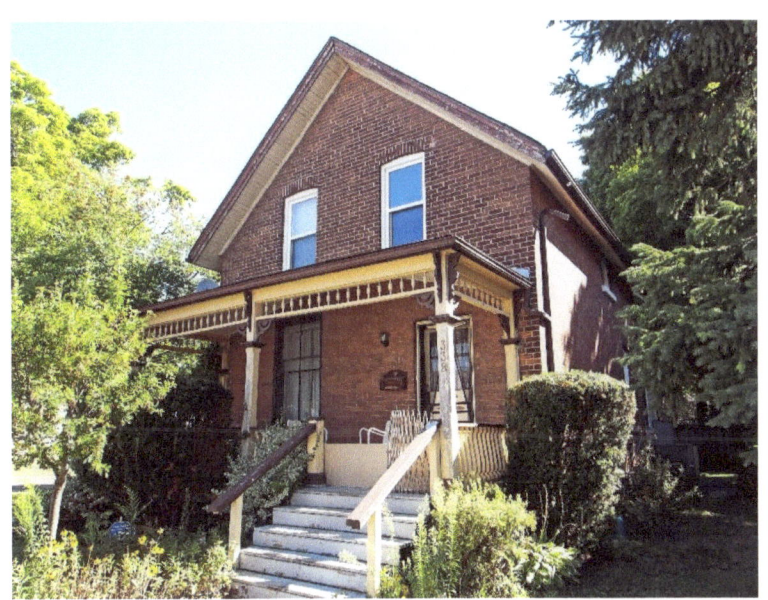

338 Mathew Street

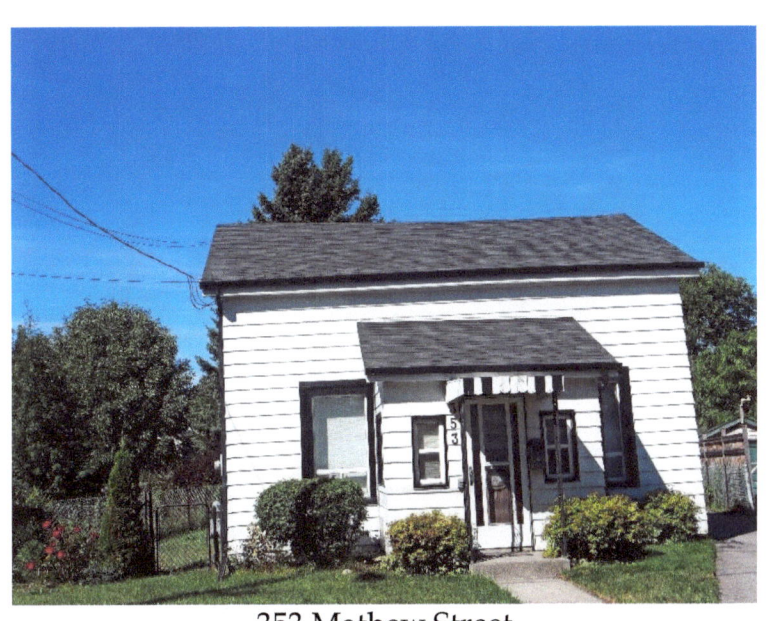

353 Mathew Street

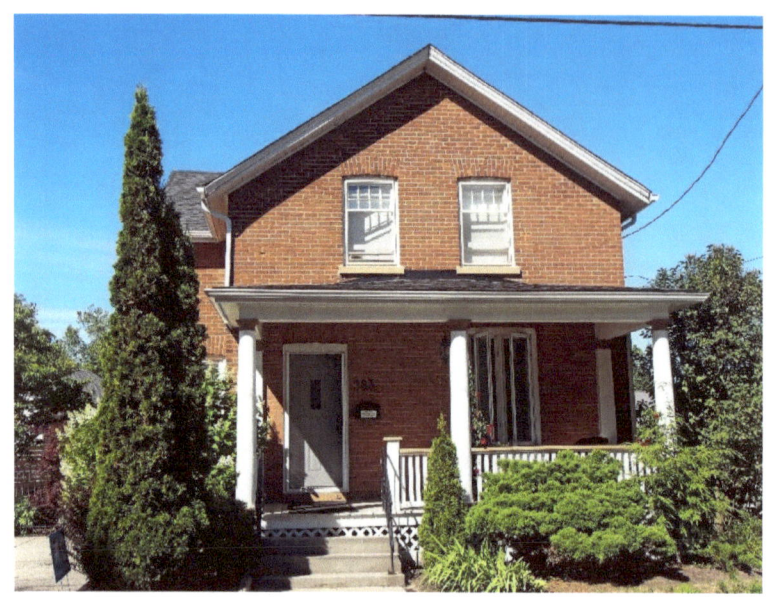

383 Mathew Street

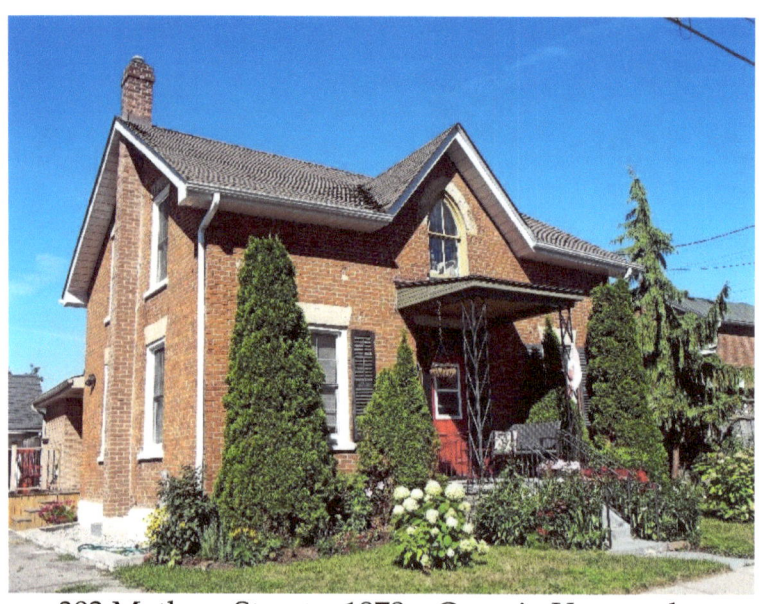

393 Mathew Street – 1878 – Ontario Vernacular

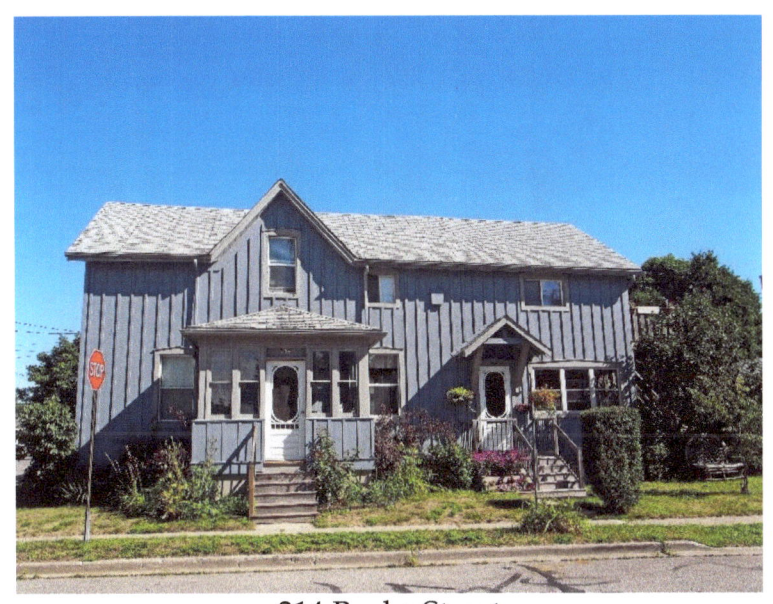

214 Burke Street

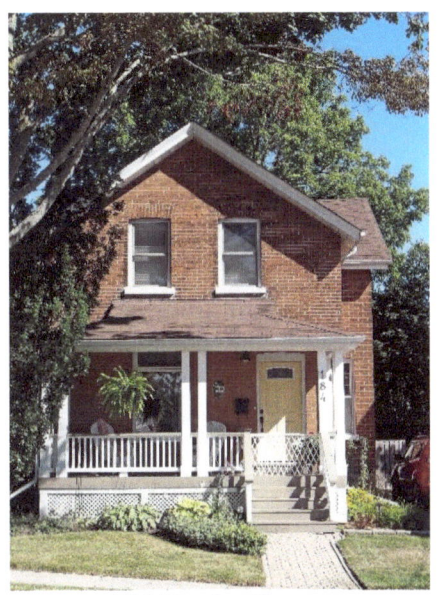

184 Burke Street

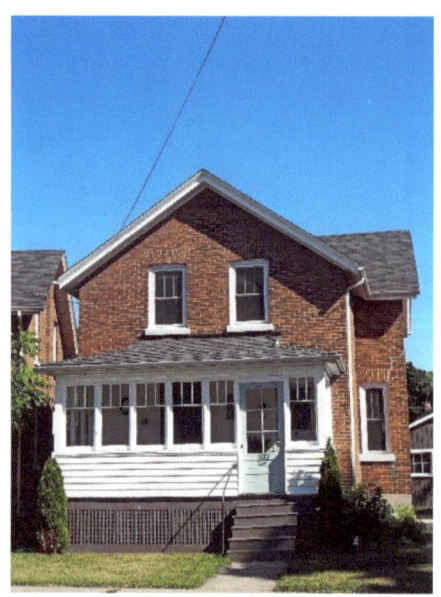

192 Burke Street

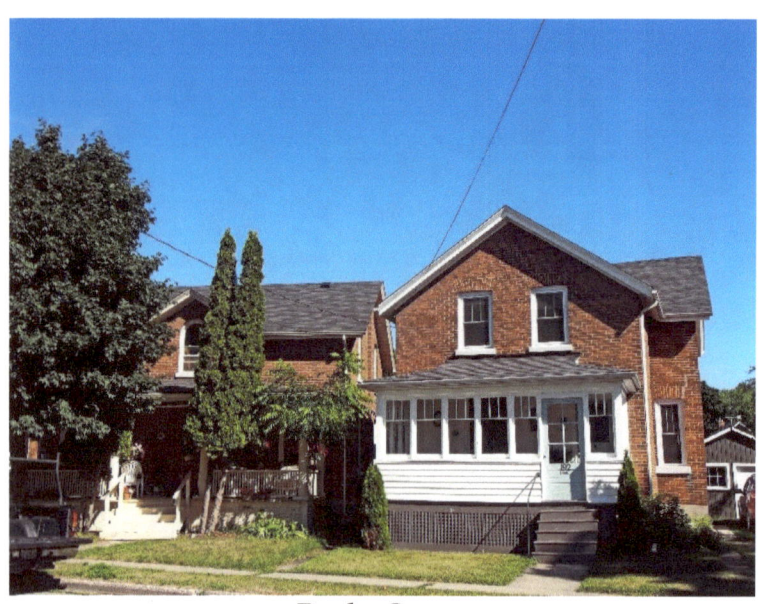

Burke Street

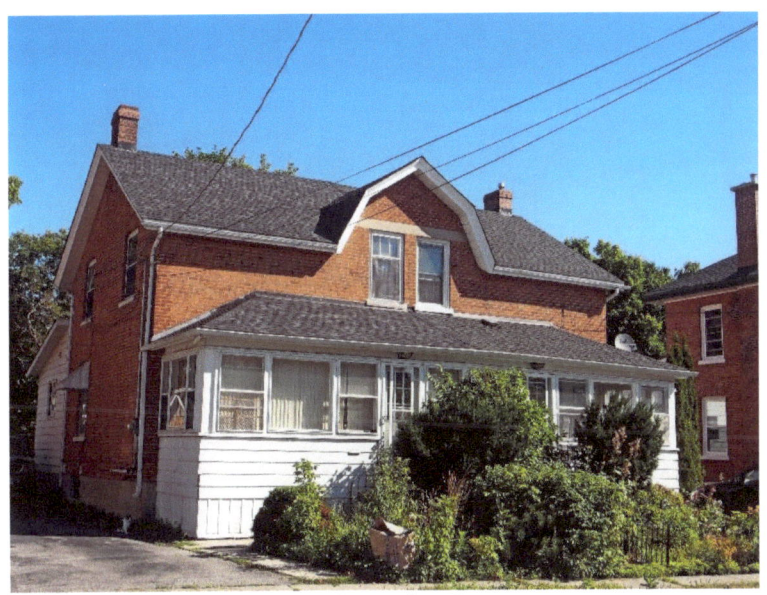

178-180 Burke Street

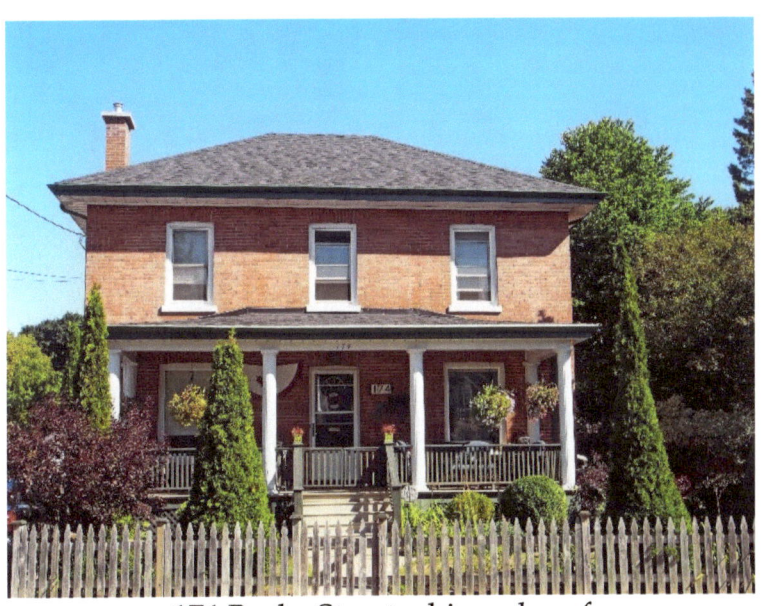

174 Burke Street – hipped roof

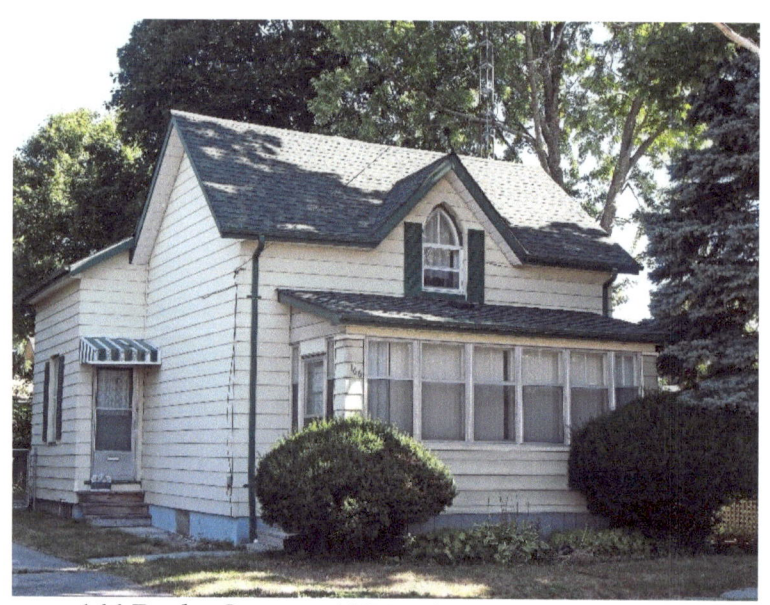

166 Burke Street – 1874 – Ontario Vernacular

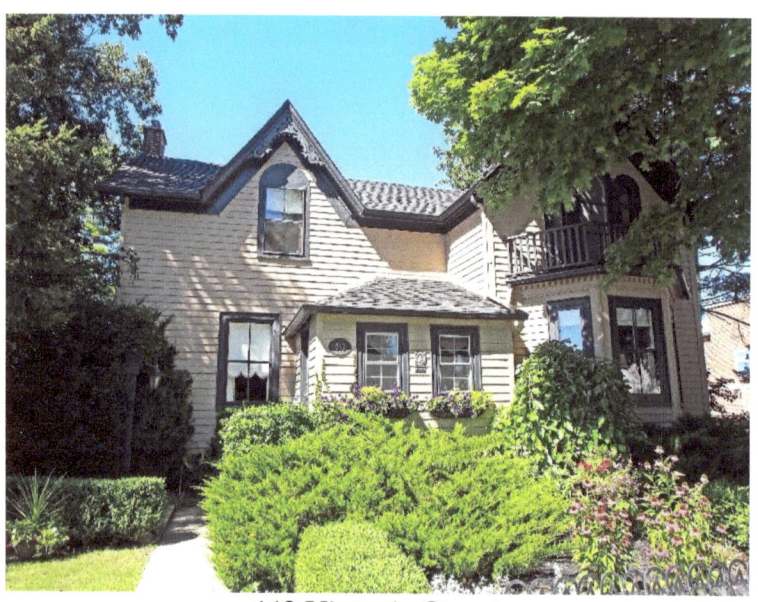

443 Victoria Street

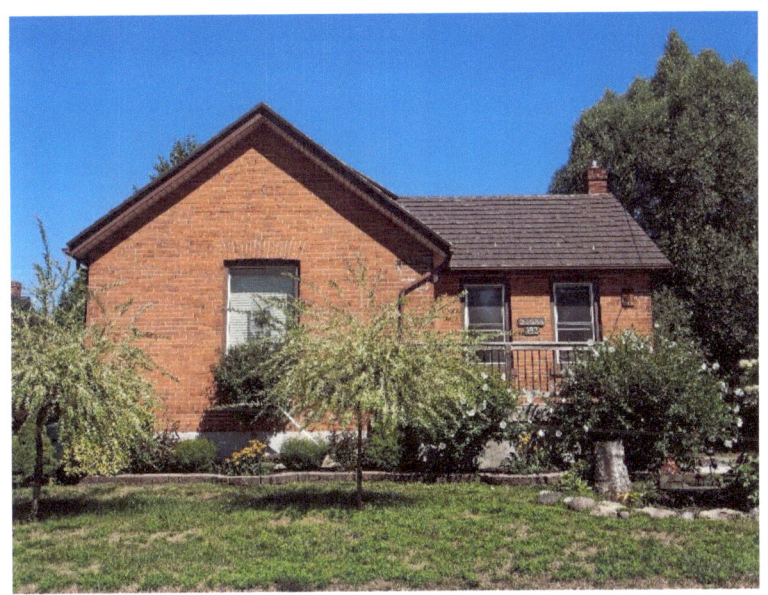

182 Furnace Street - 1852

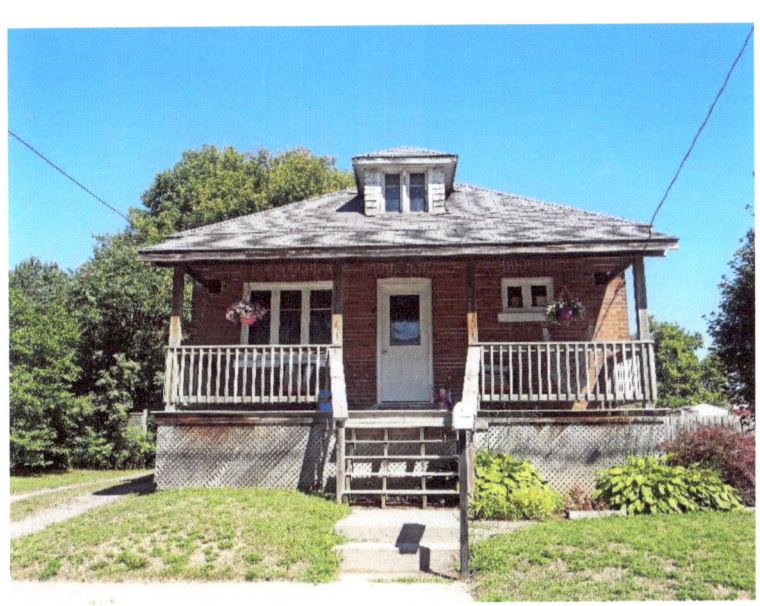

174 Furnace Street

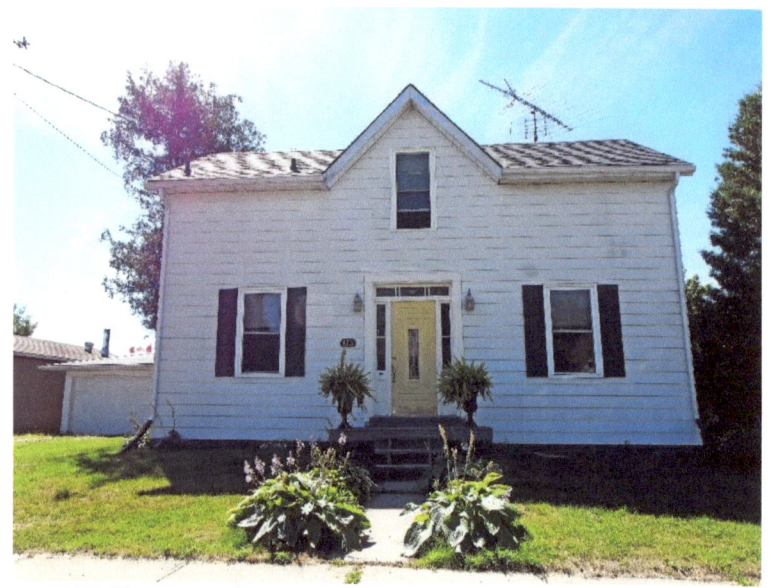

173 Furnace Street – 1870s – Ontario Vernacular

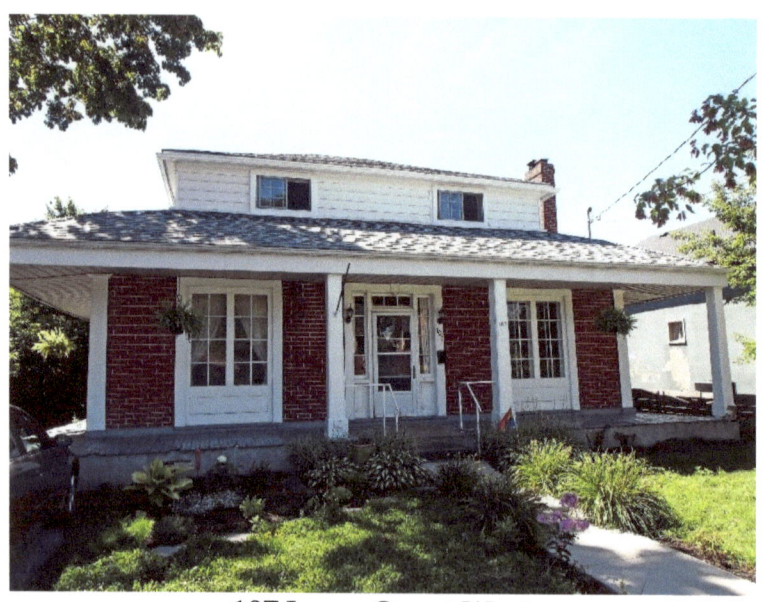

107 James Street West

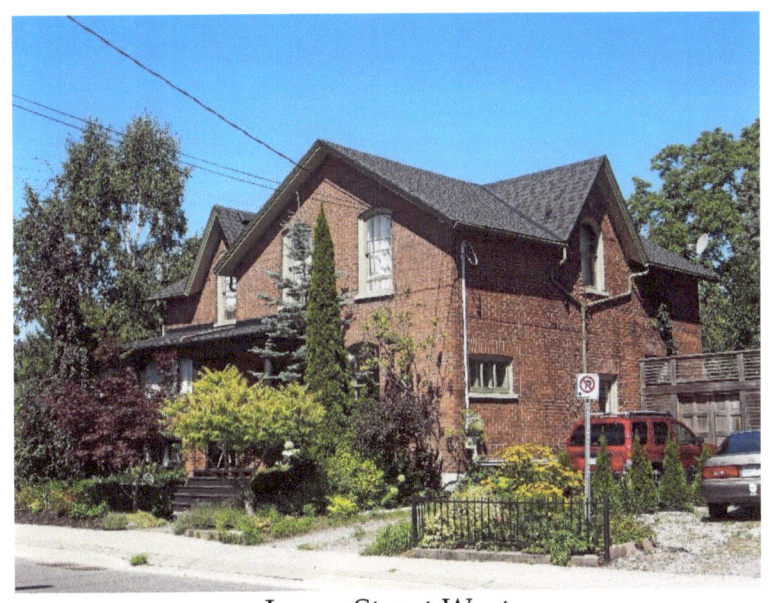

James Street West

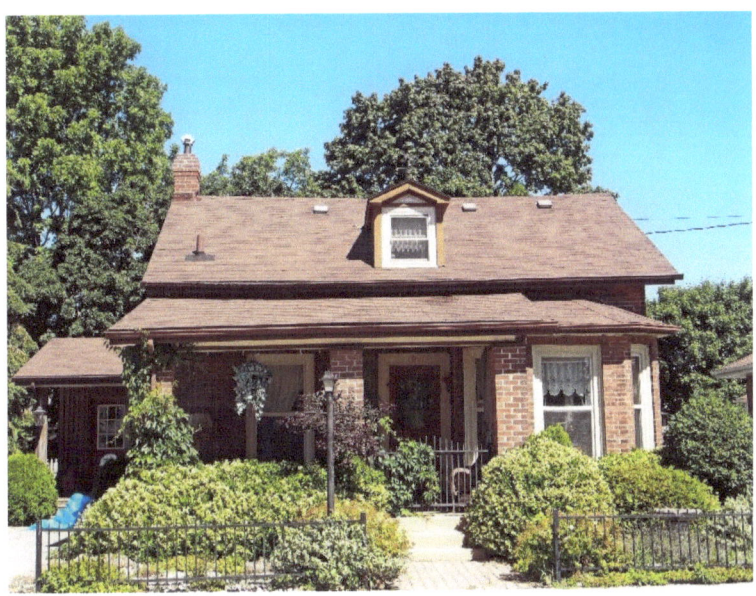

104 James Street West

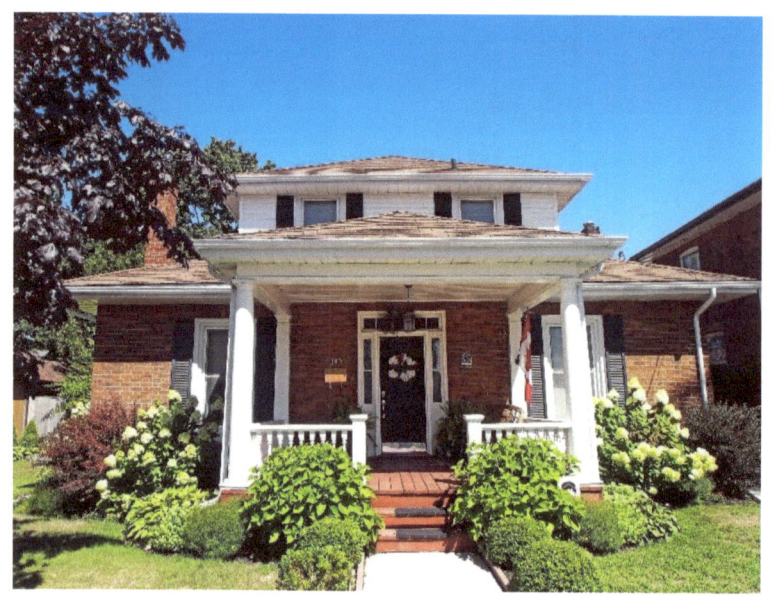

100 James Street West

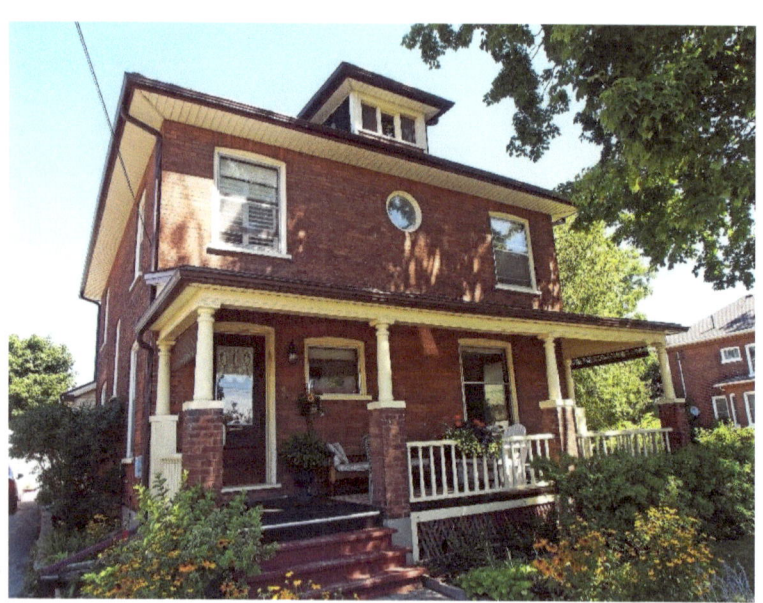

96 James Street West

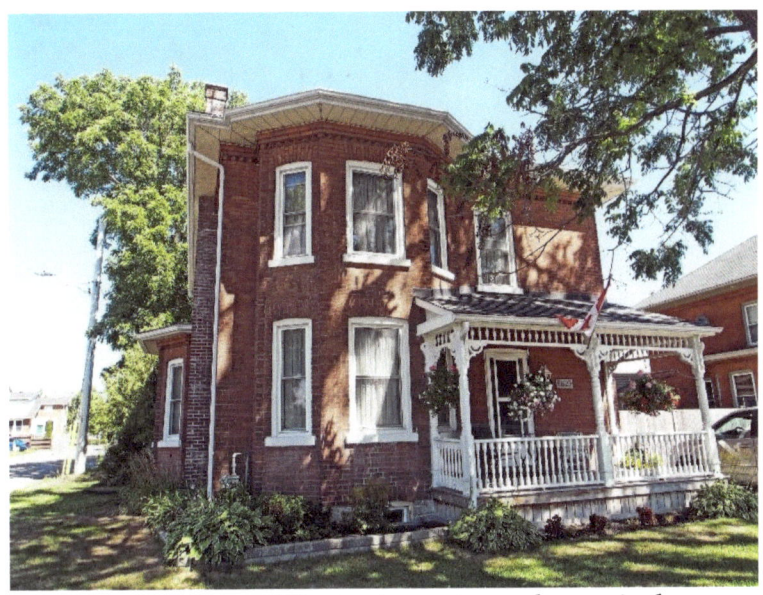

82 James Street West – two-storey bay window

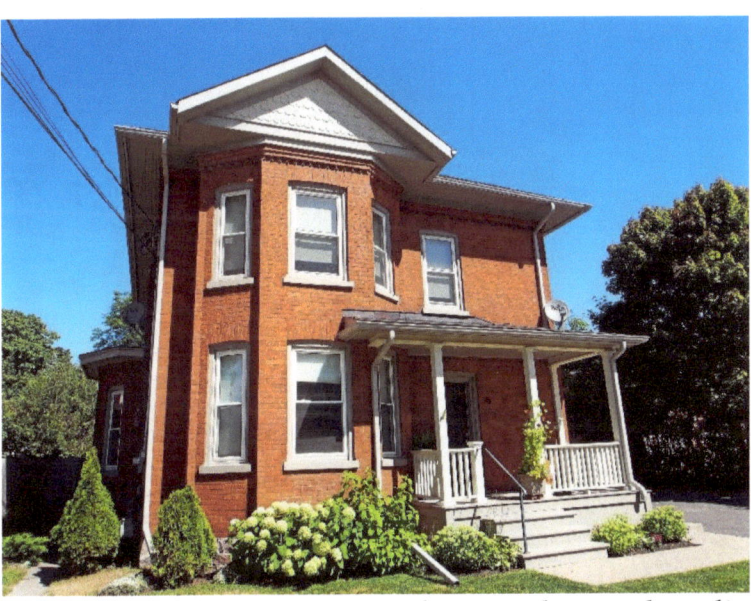

78 James Street West – two-storey bay window with pediment

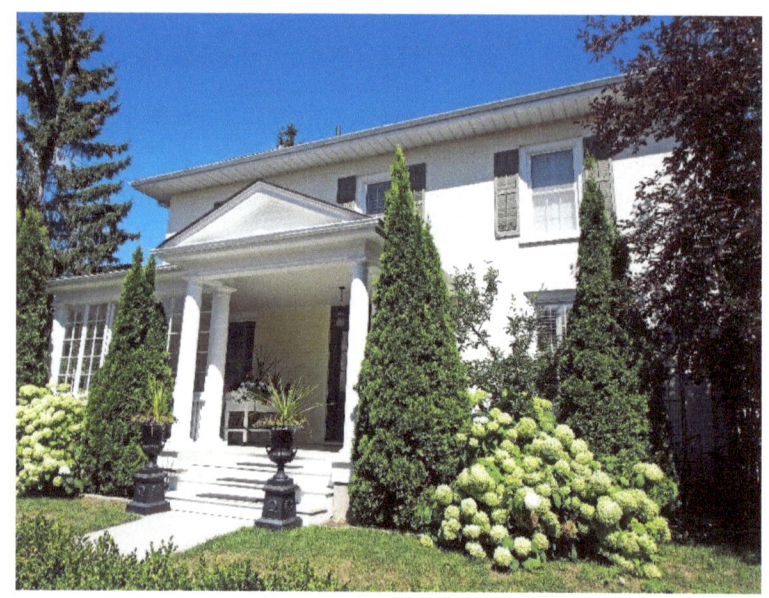

James Street West

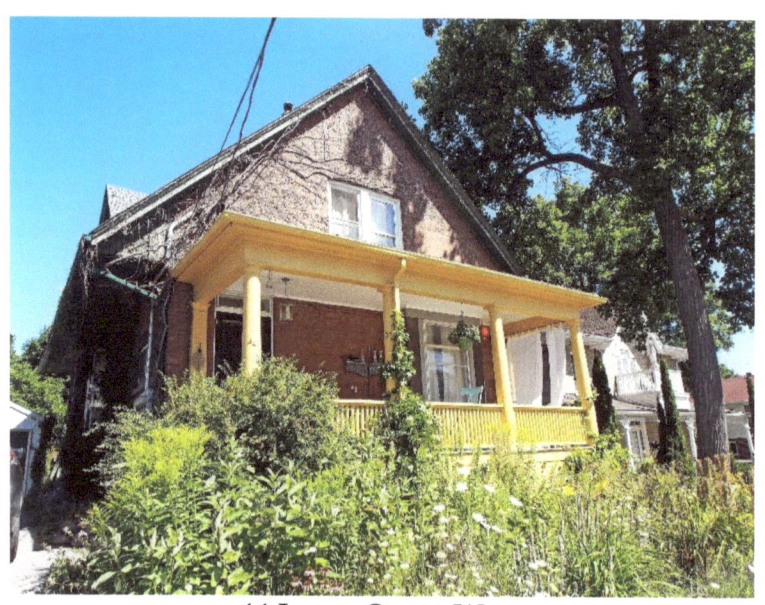

44 James Street West

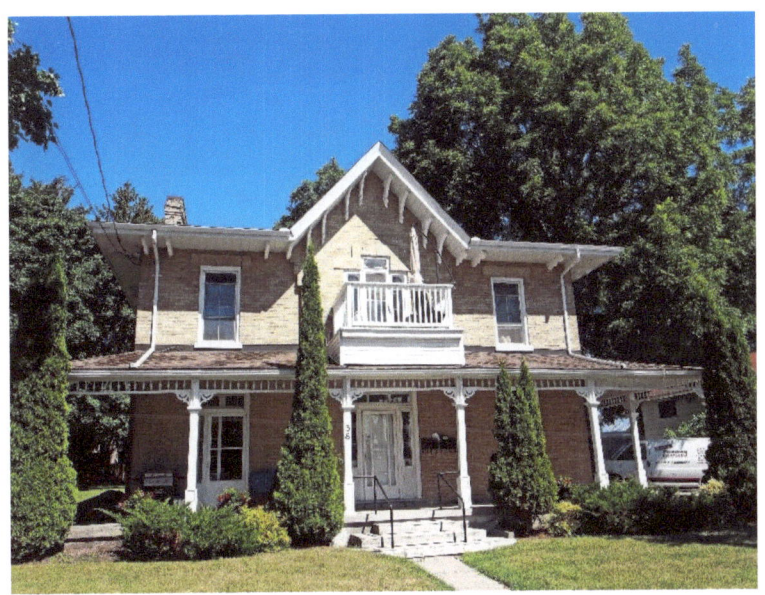

38 James Street West

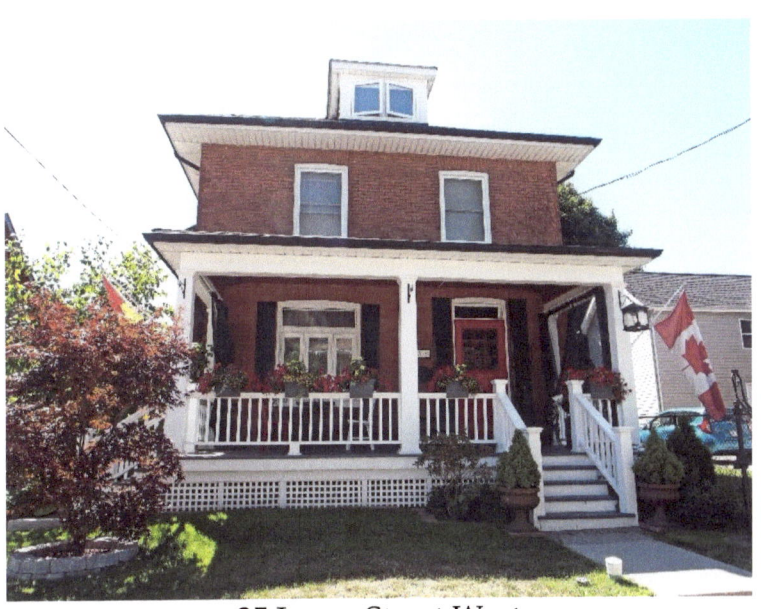

35 James Street West

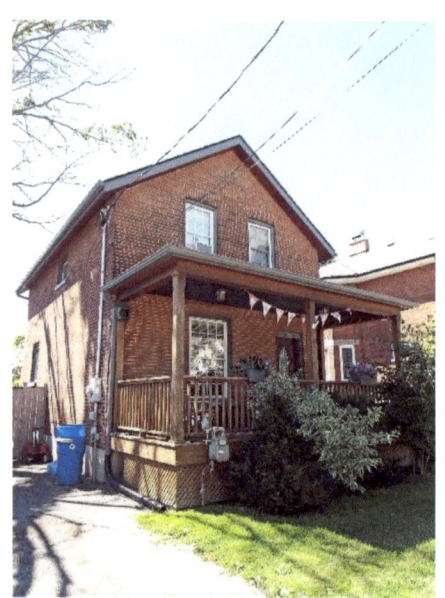

29 James Street West

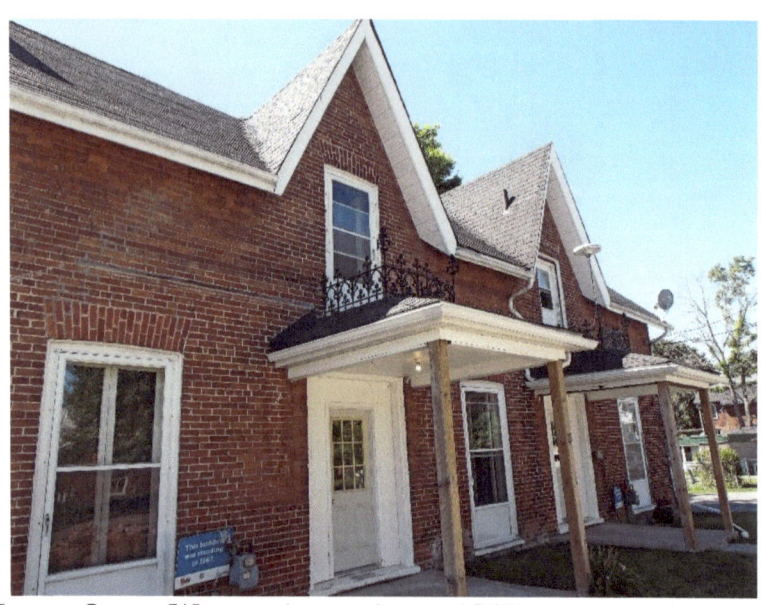

15 James Street West – circa prior to 1867 – iron cresting above entrance

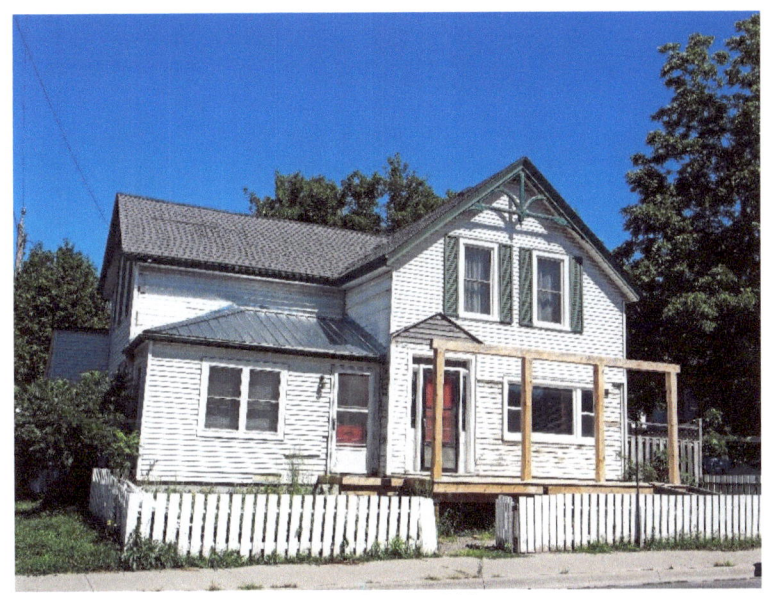

James Street West

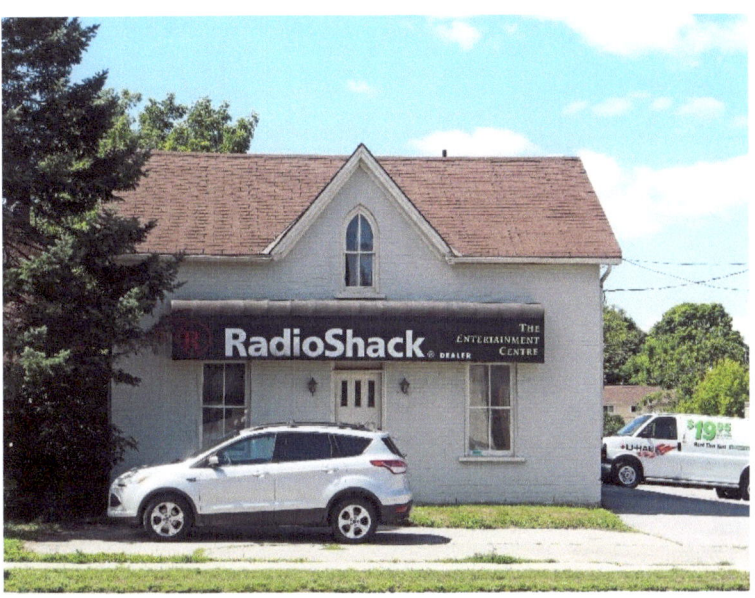

467 Division Street

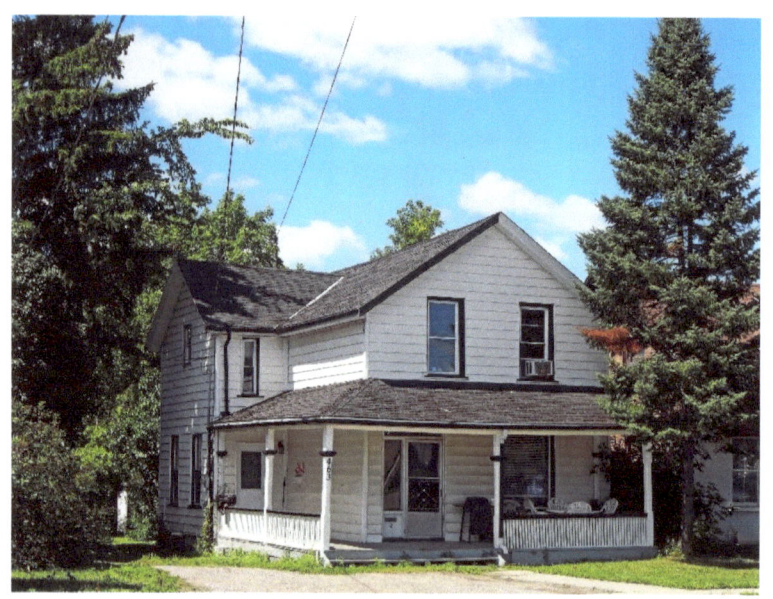

463 Division Street

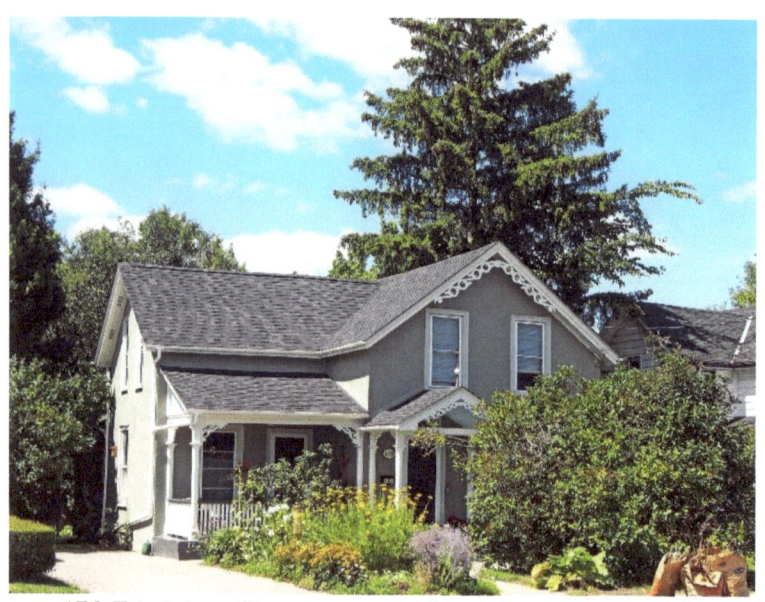

459 Division Street – verge board trim on gable

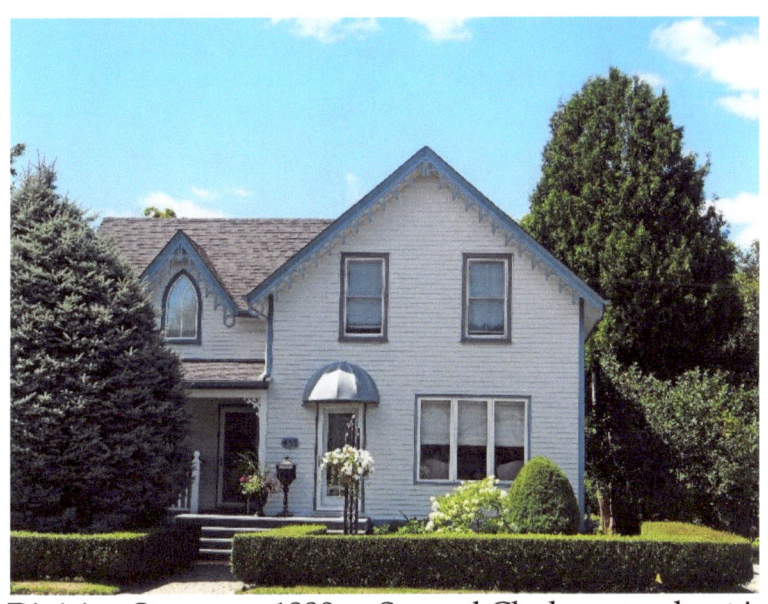

453 Division Street – c. 1880s – Samuel Clark, a merchant in Cobourg, bought this house from shoemaker John Sherman in 1884. Clapboard siding and bargeboard are the distinguishing features. There is a Gothic window in the small gable.

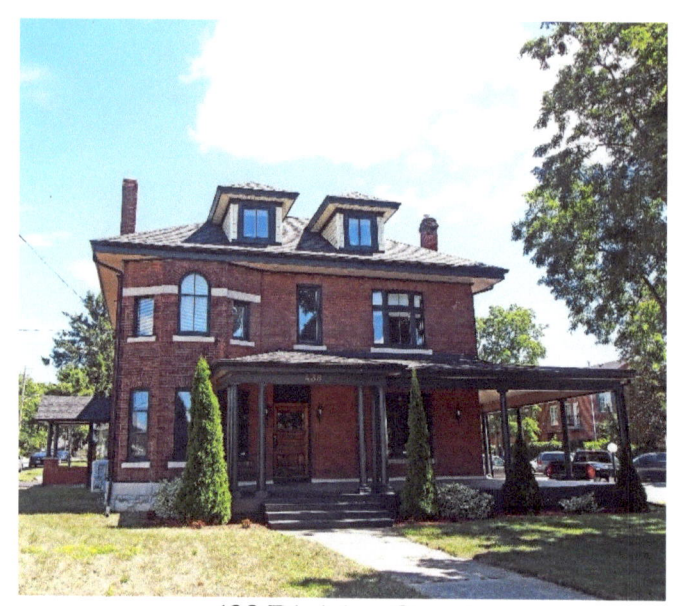

438 Division Street

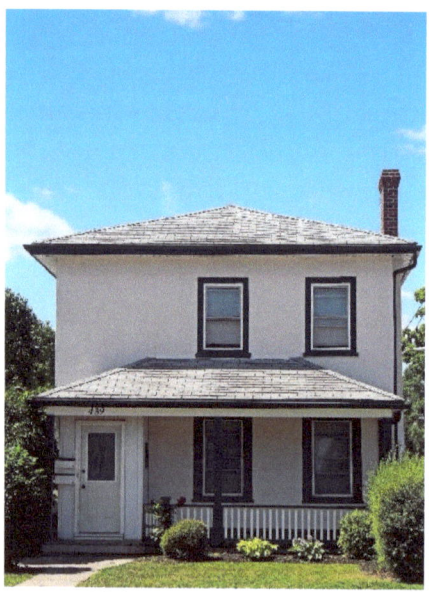

439 Division Street

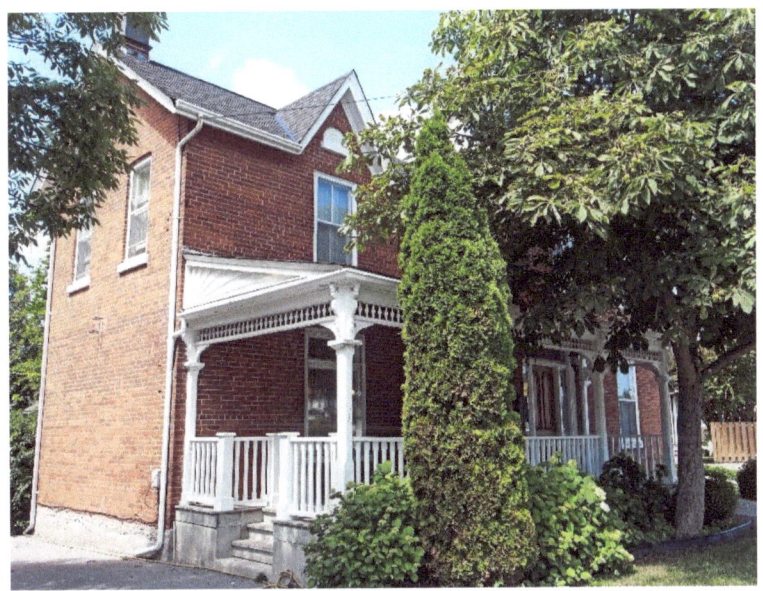

431 Division Street

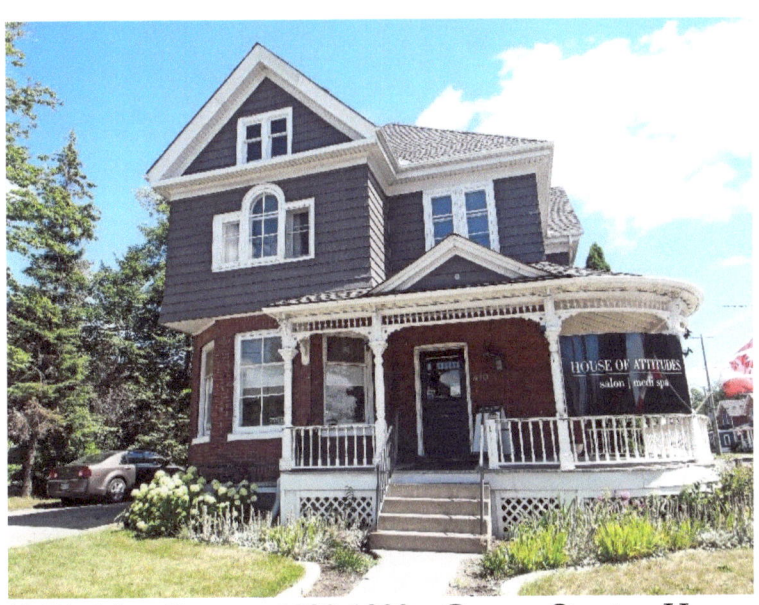

410 Division Street – 1890-1900 – George Stanton House –
Queen Anne element

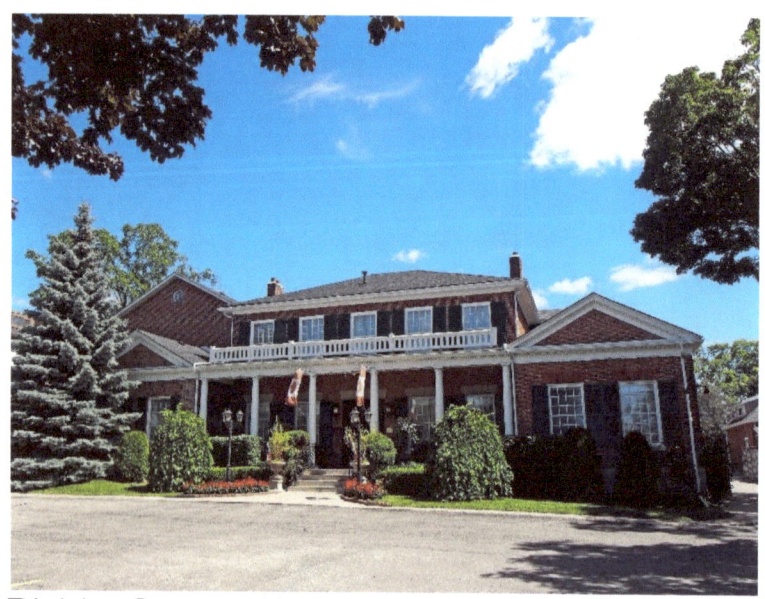

420 Division Street – 1835 – Georgian - Residence of George Perry, son of Ebenezer Perry, Chairman of the Board of Police, the first governing body of the Town. It is in Regency style with its contrasting window sizes on the first and second floors, sweeping galleries, low hip roof, and tall chimneys. It is now Woodlawn Inn.

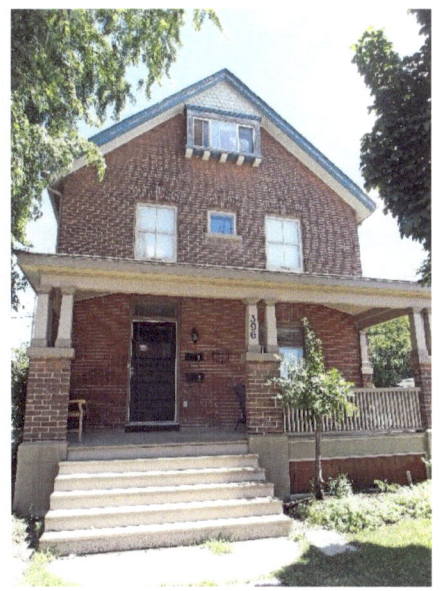

396 Division Street

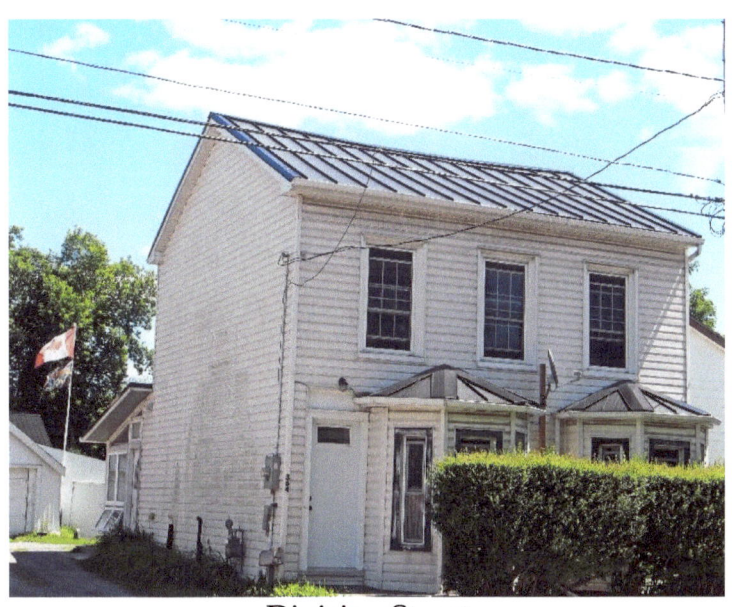

Division Street

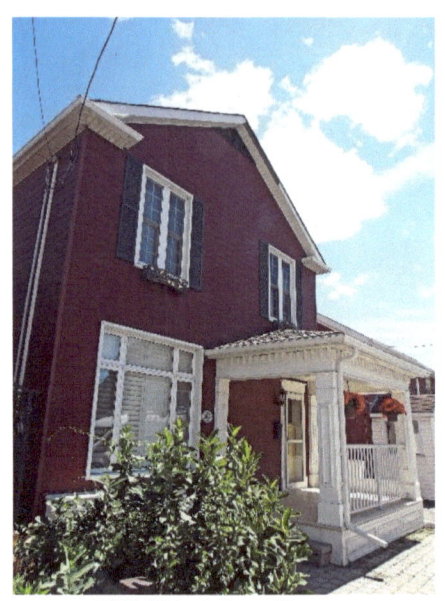

382 Division Street

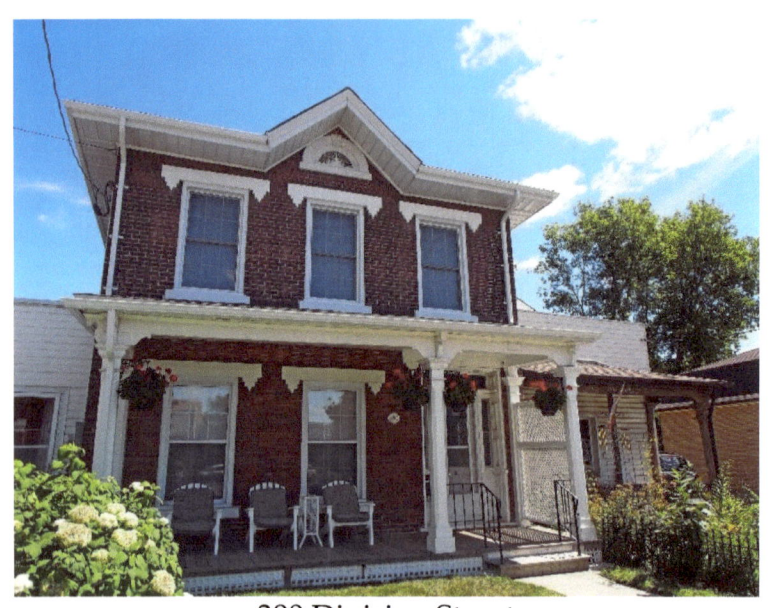

390 Division Street

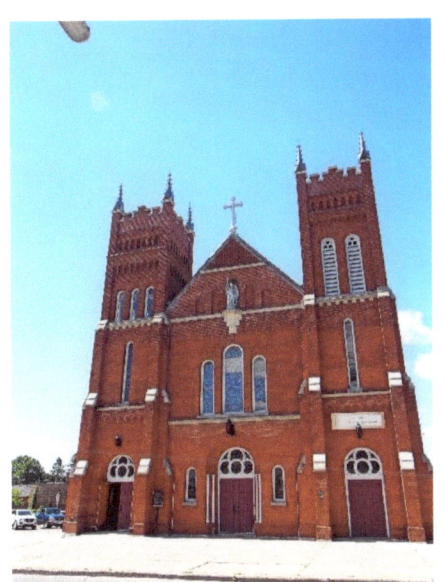

379 Division Street – St. Michael's Roman Catholic Church – c. 1895 – Romanesque Revival style, red brick, locally quarried stone foundation, the main entrance is flanked by two square bell towers each crowned by four spires – A statue of St. Michael is stationed above the front door.

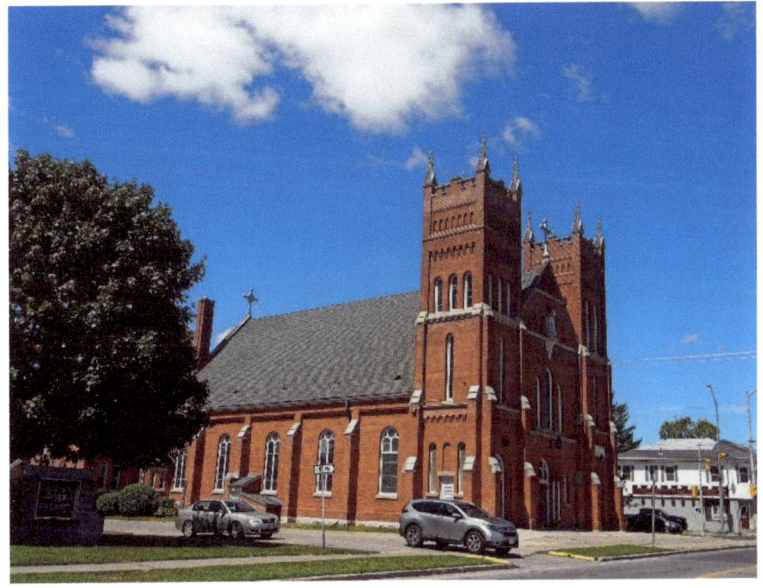

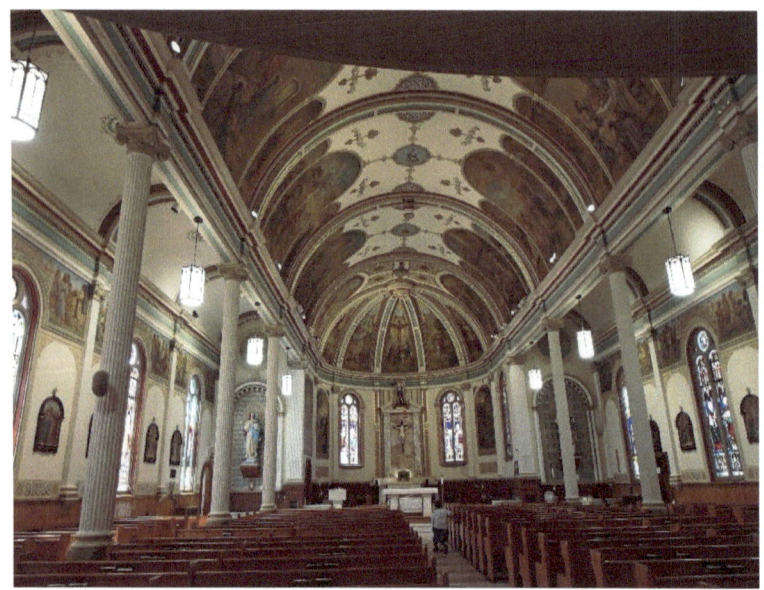

The three interior barrel-vaulted ceilings are supported by Ionic columns and matching pilasters on the side walls. Biblical history is depicted in oil paintings on the ceiling and the stations of the cross on the side walls.

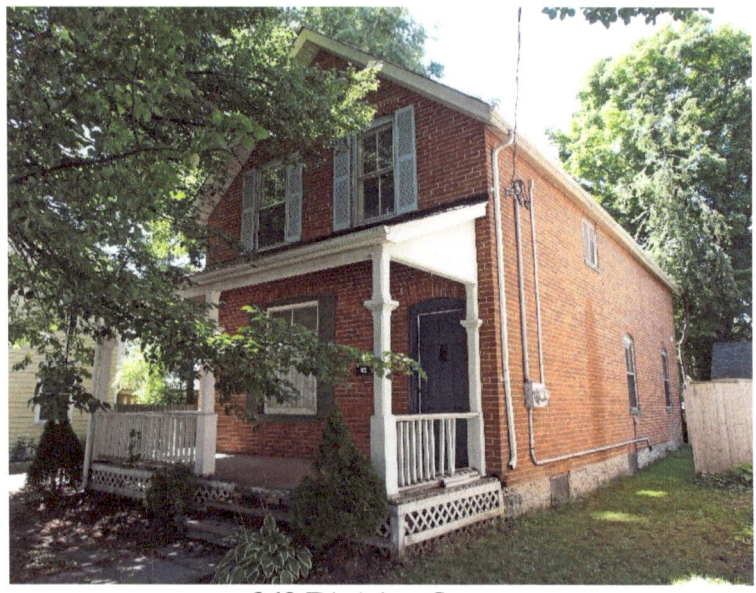

363 Division Street

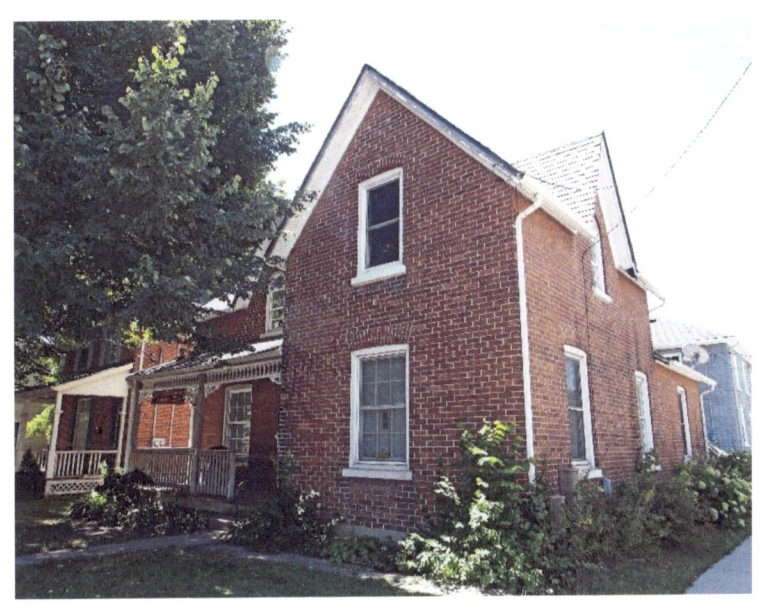

369 Division Street

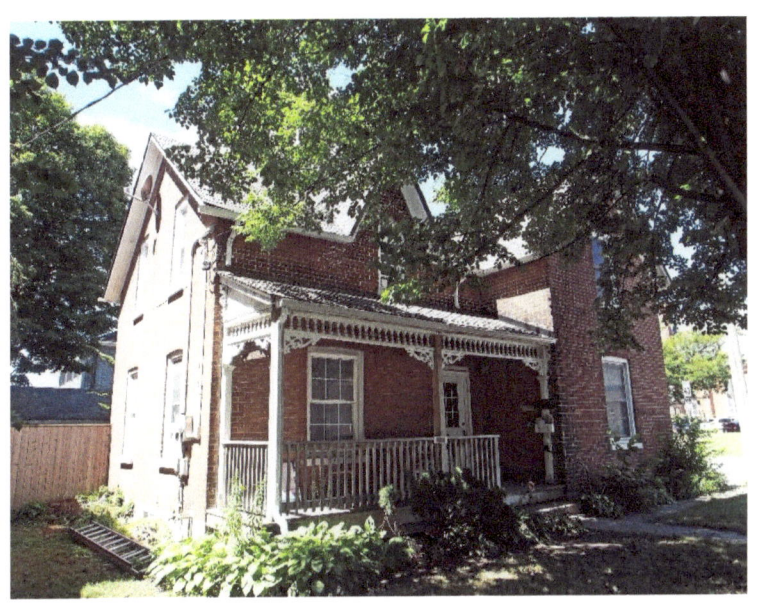

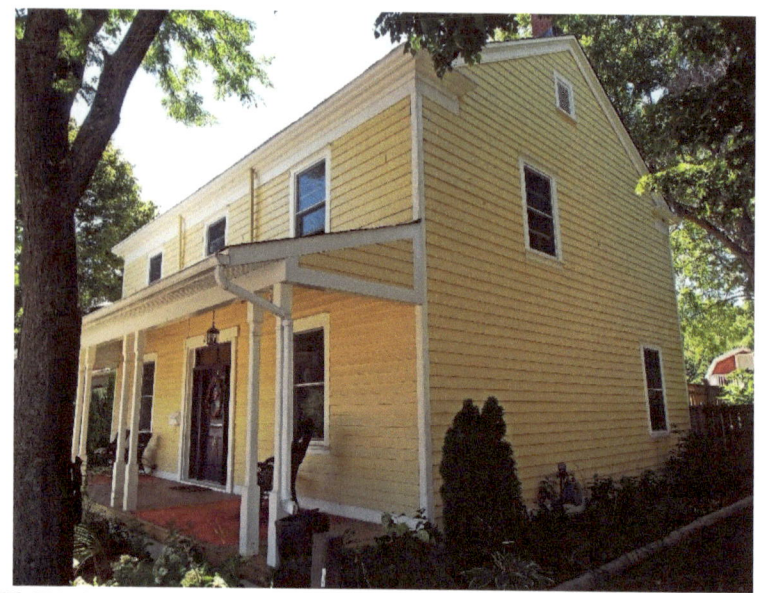

359 Division Street – 1850 - This is one of the best surviving examples of mid-nineteenth century frame construction in Cobourg. It was built by William Grieve in the Georgian style.

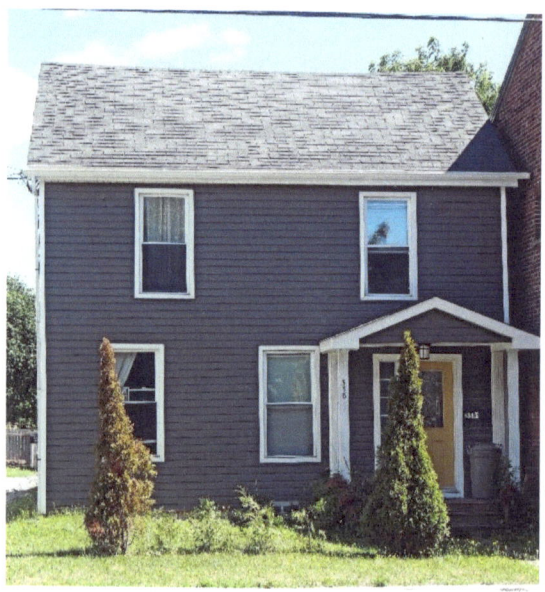

358 Division Street

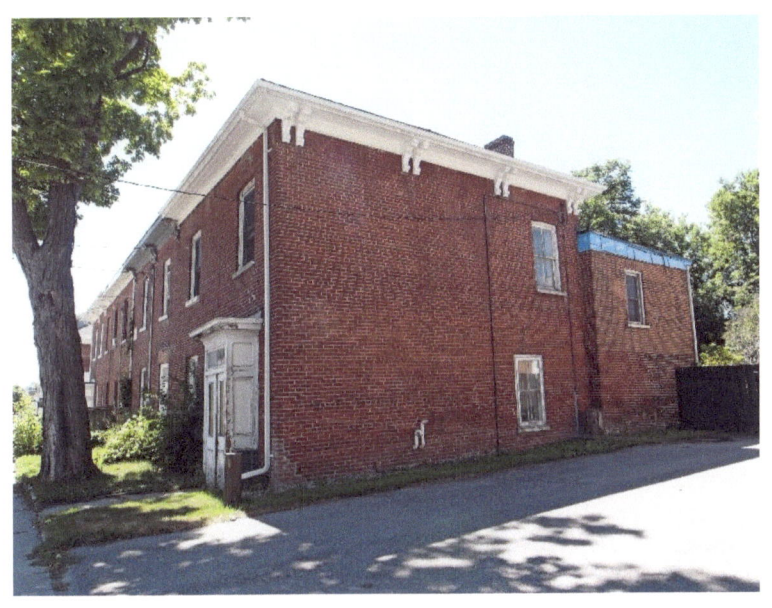

349 Division Street – paired cornice brackets

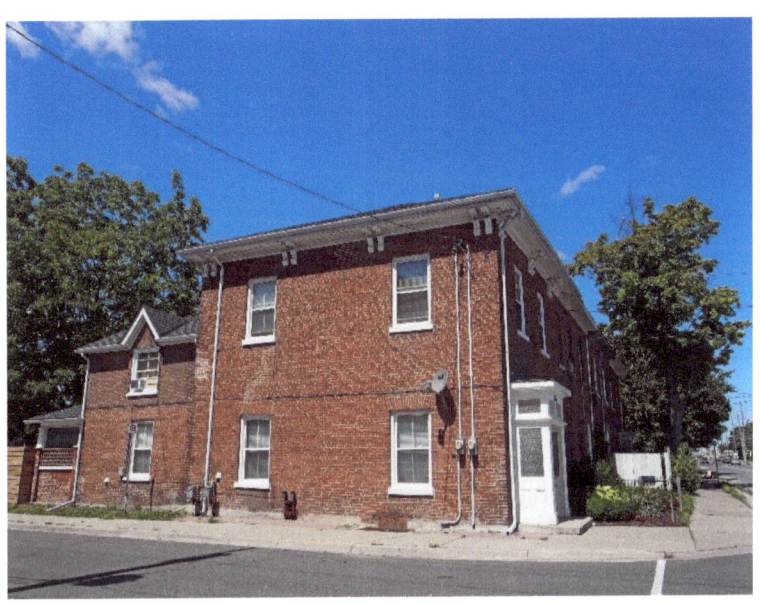

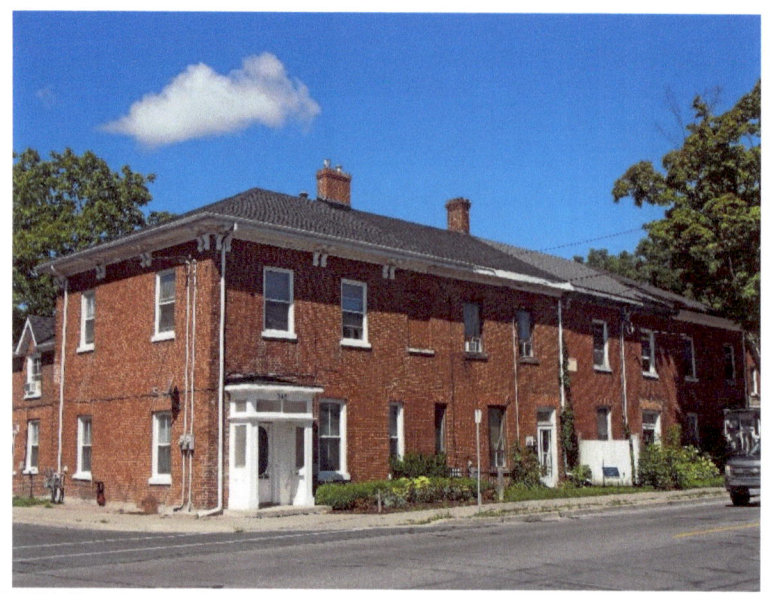

345-351 Division Street - "Campbell Terrace" - Terrace housing was not common in Cobourg, but this is the finest example. The south part was constructed in the 1850s, while the north part was added in the early 1870s.

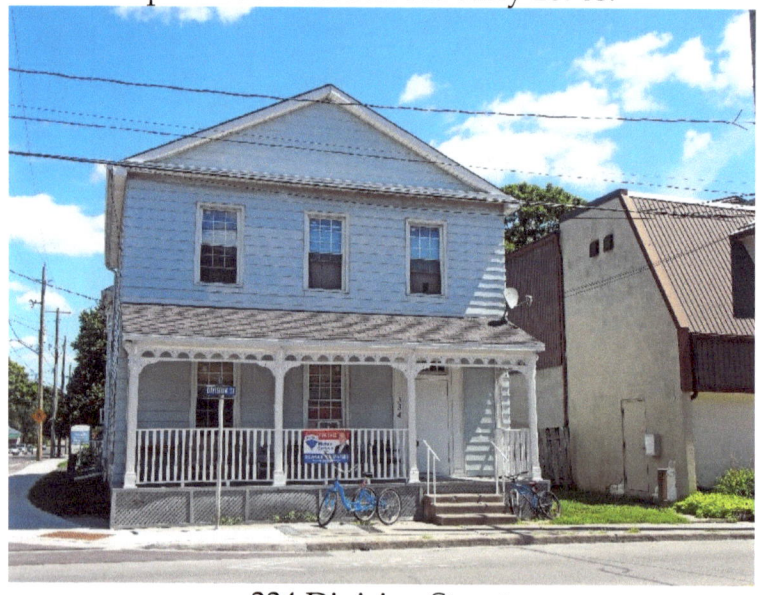

334 Division Street

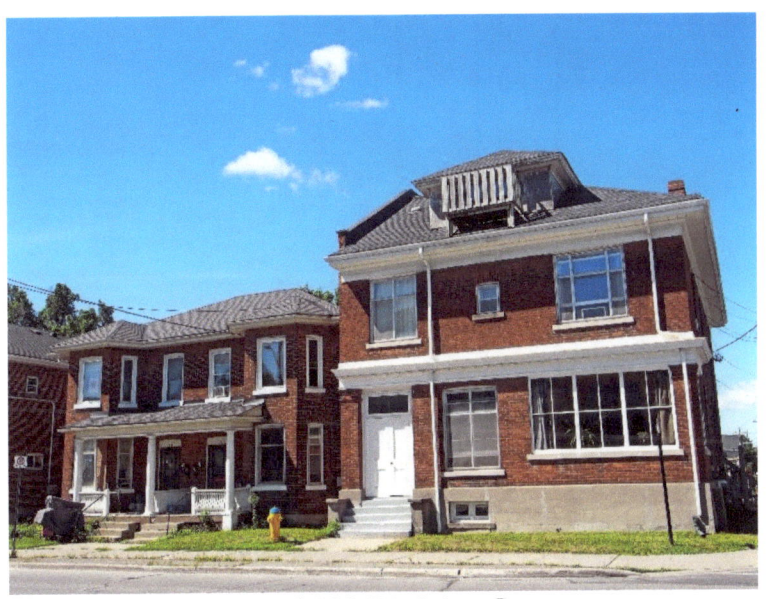

327 and 329 Division Street

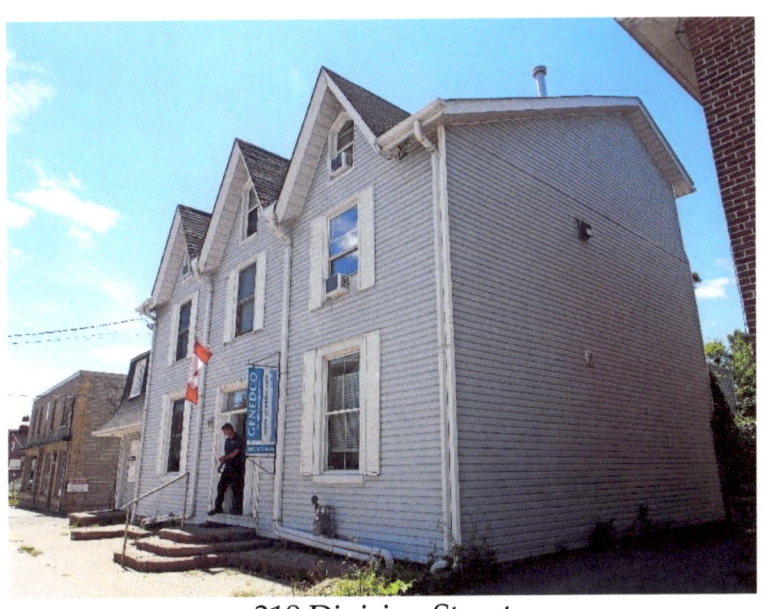

319 Division Street

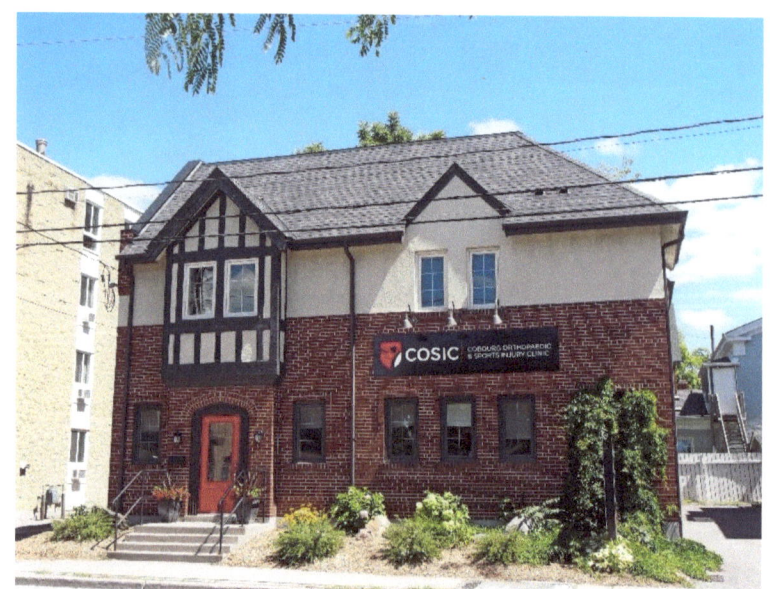
304 Division Street – Tudor half-timbering

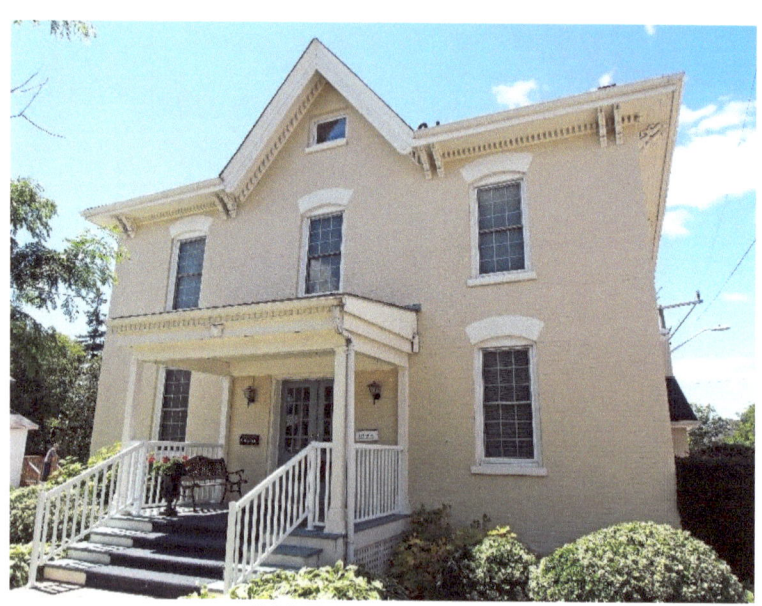
301 Division Street

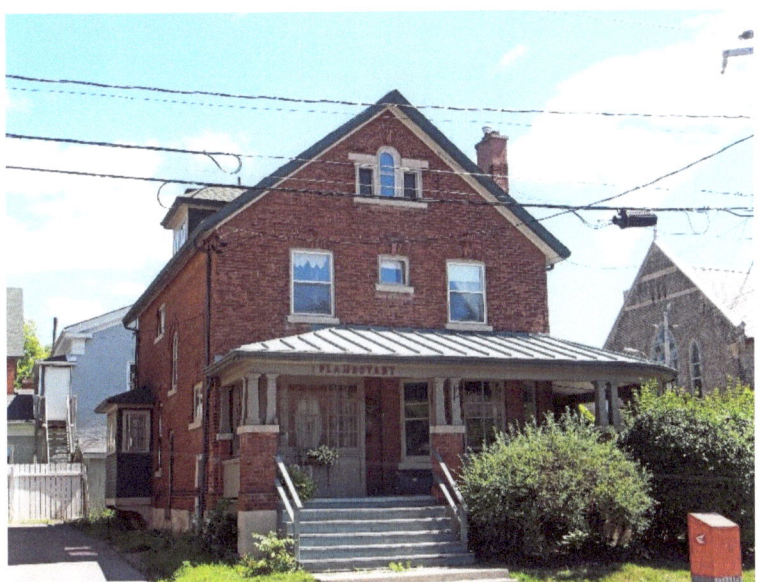

300 Division Street – 1870 – 2½ storey – Palladian-type window in gable

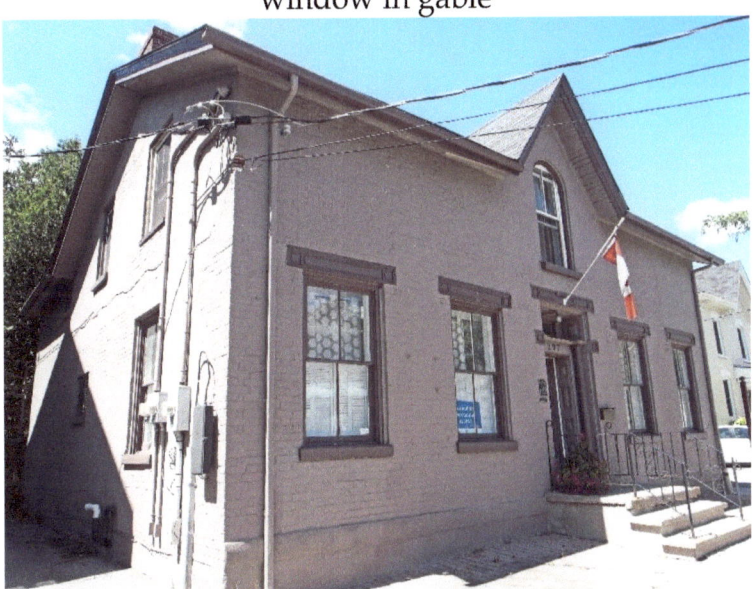

297 Division Street - c. 1842 - Dr. James Gilchrist built this house as his office and residence. Gilchrist's brother John was the first physician licensed in Upper Canada.

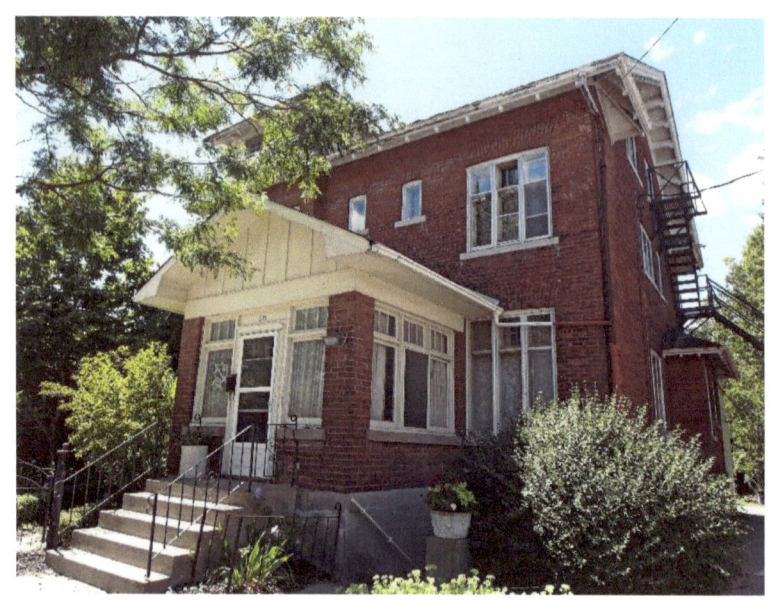

291 Division Street

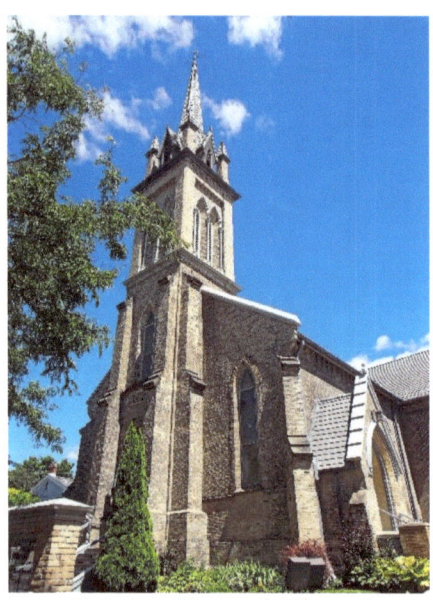

284 Division Street - Trinity United Church – c. 1852 – Gothic – lancet windows, buttresses

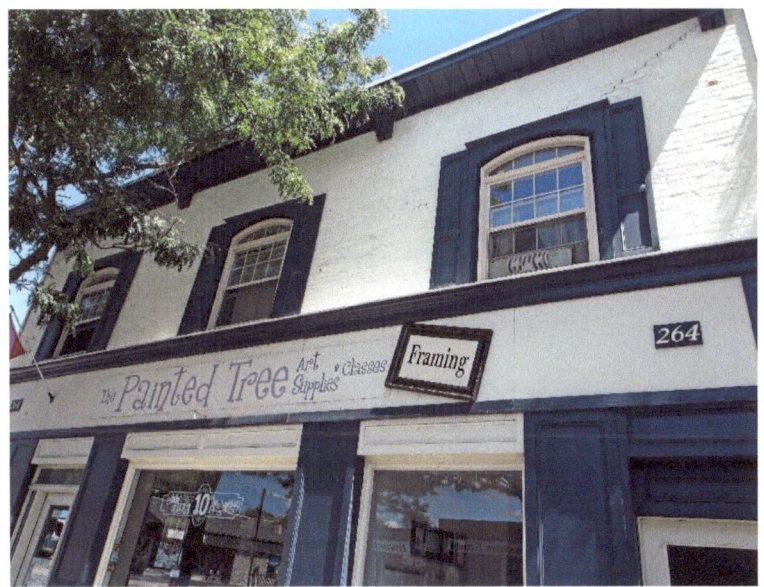

264 Division Street

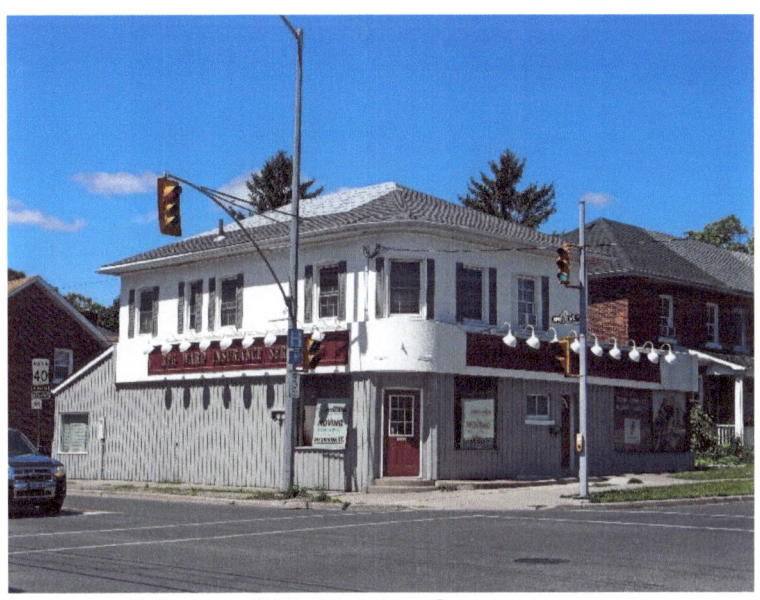

247 Division Street

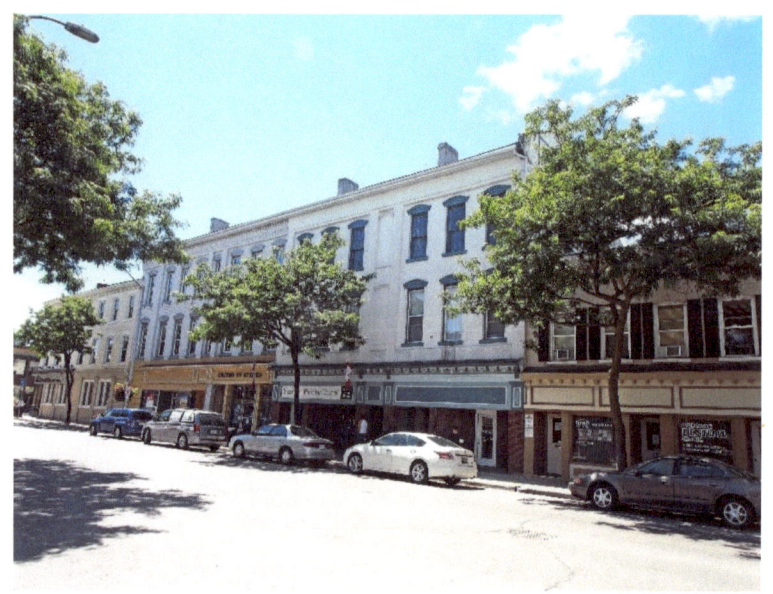

Division Street

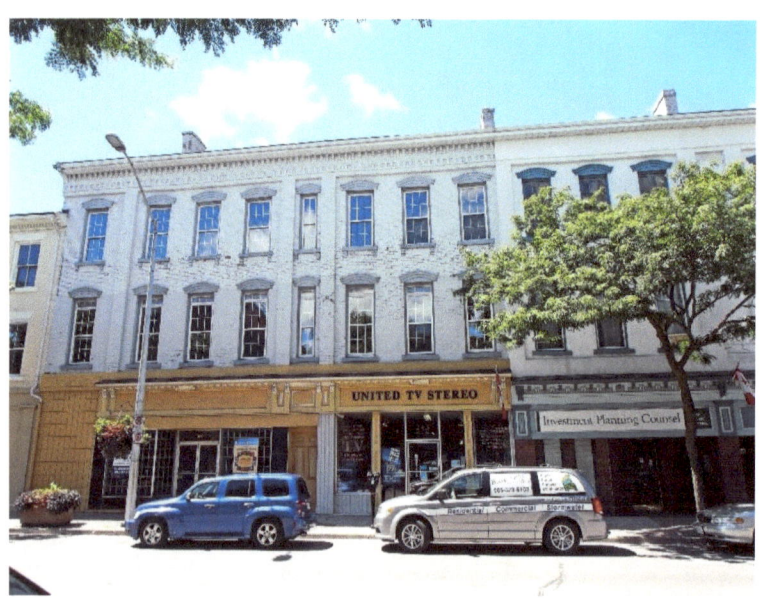

Division Street

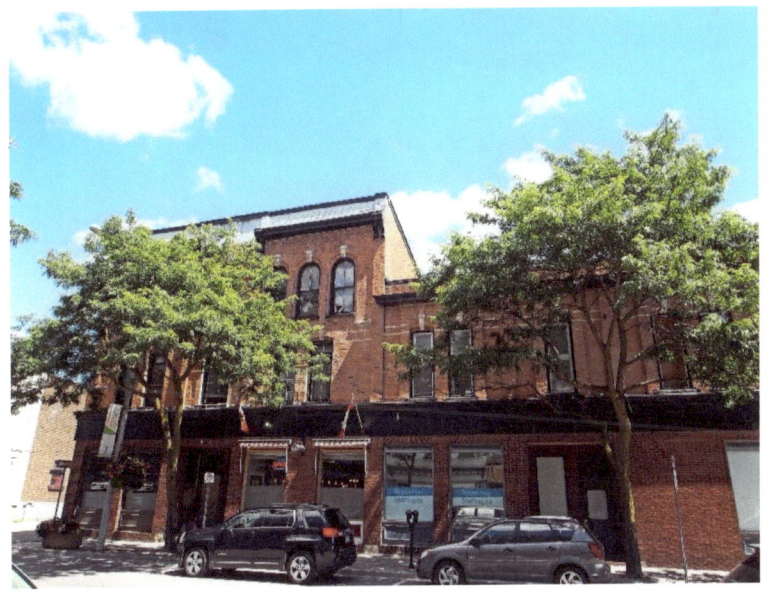

Division Street

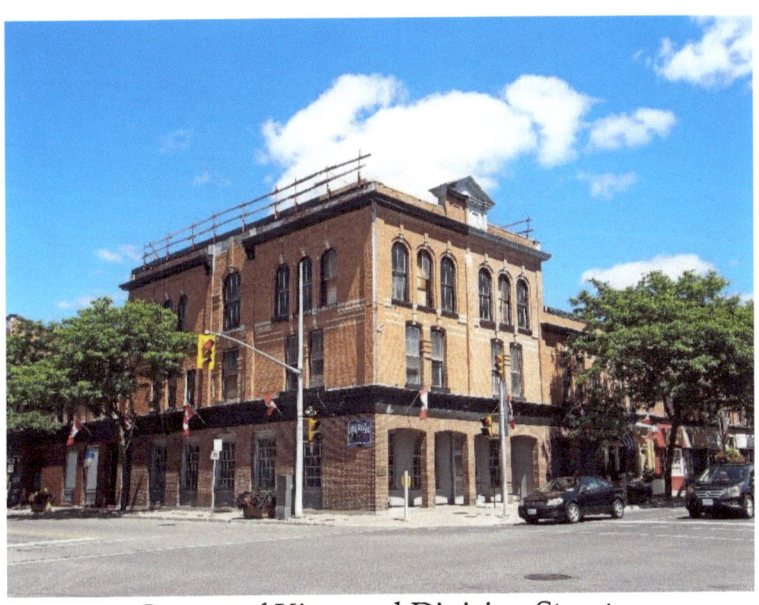

Corner of King and Division Streets

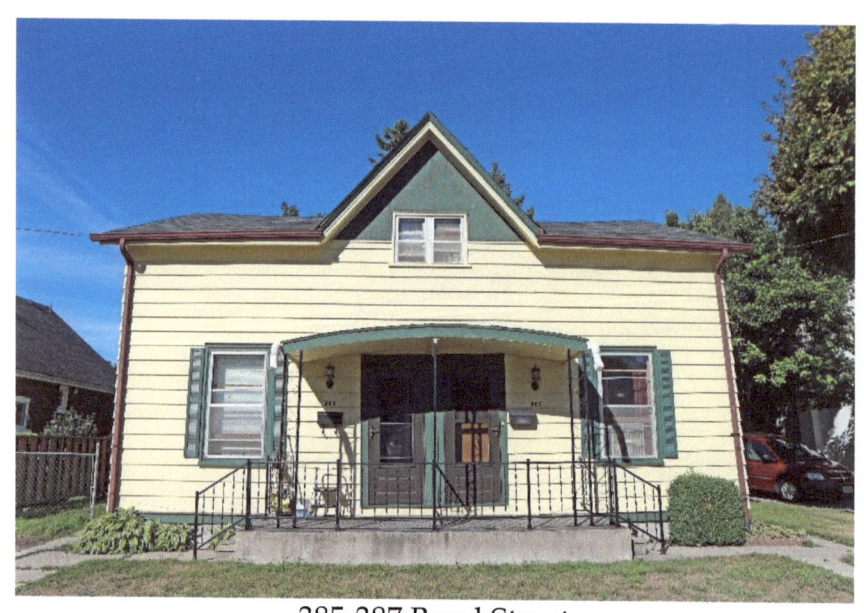

385-387 Bond Street

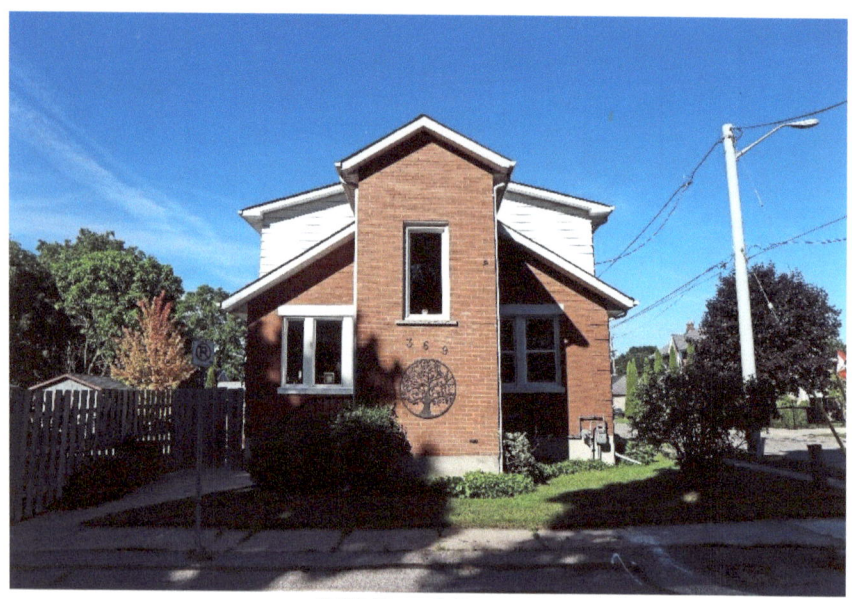

369 Bond Street

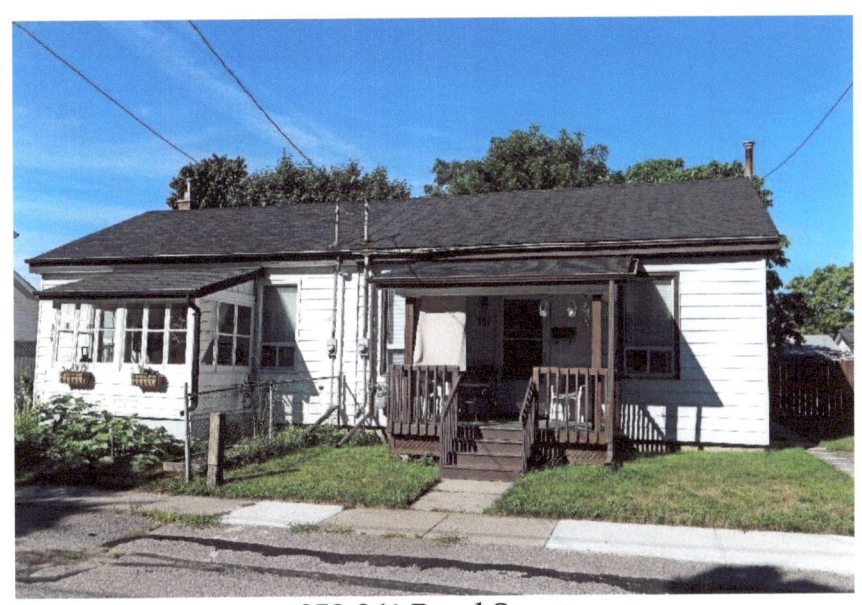

359-361 Bond Street

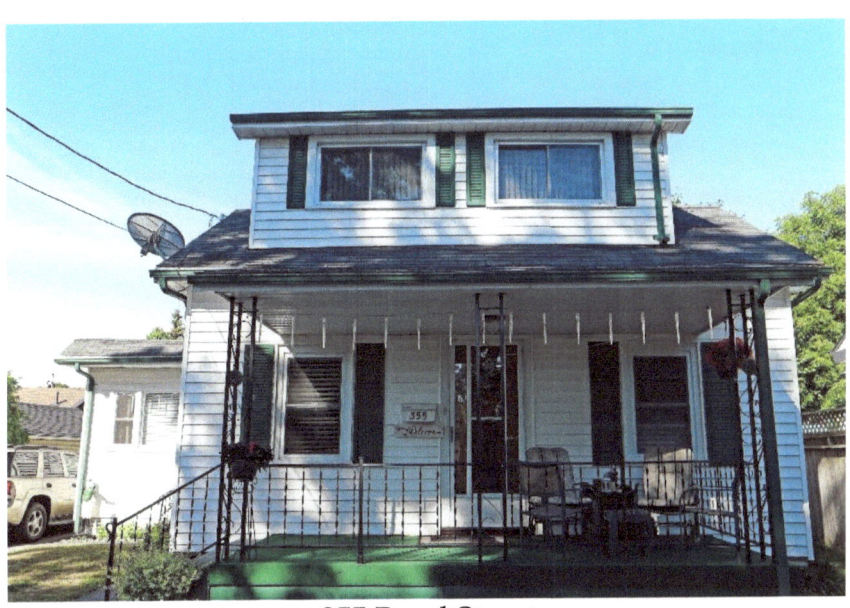

355 Bond Street

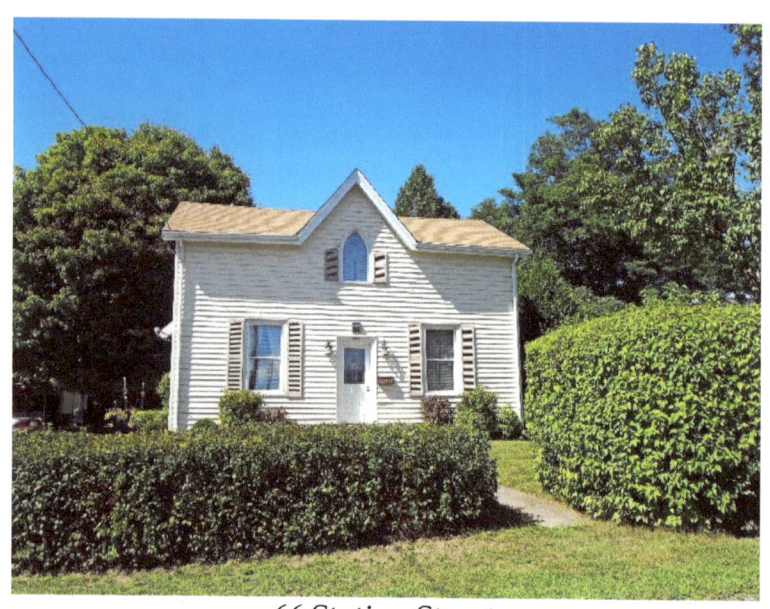

66 Station Street

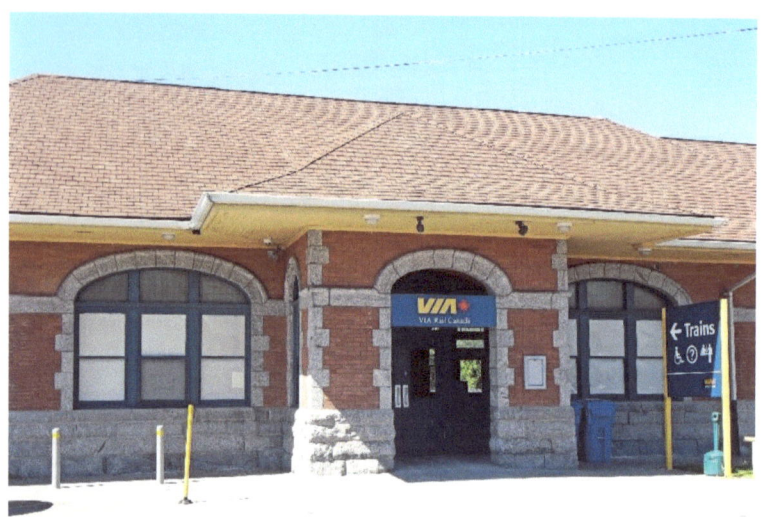

530-532 George Street - Via Train Station - 1911

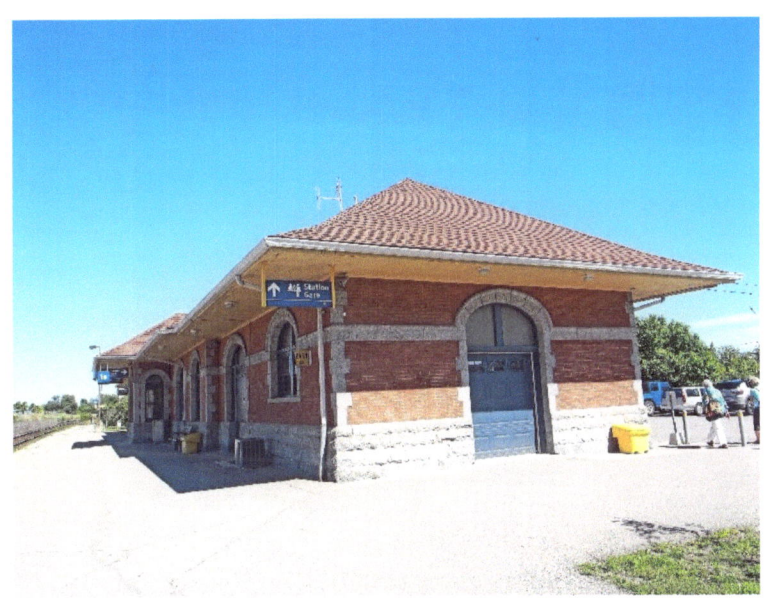

Cobourg was fortunate to be located on the mainline of the Grand Trunk Railway, which by 1859 stretched all the way from Portland, Maine to Chicago. This substantial building was constructed in the Romanesque style and, completely restored in 1993, still continues its original role as the VIA passenger station.

The Canadian government formed the Canadian National Railway in 1917. By 1923 it had absorbed the Canadian Northern, Grand Trunk Pacific, National Transcontinental and Intercolonial Railways, and several smaller railway companies. The CNR operated a passenger service through Cobourg along the Toronto-Montreal corridor. This was maintained until the creation of Via Rail Canada as a separate Crown corporation in 1978. In the mid-1980s, the rail line to Cobourg harbor was removed from service, ending a marine-rail link that had existed for 125 years.

Other Books by Barbara Raue

Coins of Gold
Arrows, Indians and Love
The Life and Times of Barbara
The Cromwell Family Book
Laura Secord Discovered
Daddy Where Are You?

Montana Series
Book 1: Montana Dream
Book 2: Life on the Montana Frontier
Book 3: Montana to Boston and Back
Book 4: Montana Sons Go to War
Book 5: Montana Sons Return from War

Visit Barbara's website to view all of her books
http://barbararaue.ca

www.ingramcontent.com/pod-product-compliance
Lightning Source LLC
Chambersburg PA
CBHW041212180526
45172CB00016B/107